OUR WORLD

A Country-by-Country Guide

Millie Miller

SCHOLASTIC REFERENCE

An imprint of

SCHOLASTIC

Thanks for traveling with me
and helping me along the way.

My "very own"...
Ivan, Scott and Jonathan Miller

The "Digressions"...
Cyndi Nelson, Joanne Tilley,
and Sabra Dunham

Boulder Public Health . . .
Heath Harmon, Chana Goussettis,
Helen Majzler, Julie Handy, Pat Hood,
Caroline Bargman, Alex Perez, Linda Ray,
Audrey Ambler, Jean Dinwiddie,
Claire Betcher, Helen Kraft,
and Maureen McCarthy

My French connections . . .
Sarah Charre, Frederic Lechenault
and Julien Cortial

My lifeline at Scholastic . . .
Brenda Murray and Mary Jones

and friends . . .
Scott Thorburn, Barb and Charles Elbot,
Mardy Harrold, Ana San Juan,
Ben & Rafael Senterfit, and Amy Kilbride

Dedicated to the children of the world

Learning
about each
other...
helps
us to be
friends!
Ivan J. Miller

and to Machu Picchu, my favorite place.

*   *   *

Copyright © 2006 by Millie Miller

Library of Congress Cataloging-in-Publication Data available

0-439-55004-1

10 9 8 7 6 5 4 3 2 1   06 07 08 09 10

Composition by Kay Petronio

Printed in Mexico   49
First printing, October 2006

Contents

North America

North America is the third-largest continent. It includes Canada, the United States, Mexico, Central America, the Caribbean, and Greenland.

At 20,320 feet (6,194 m) tall, Mount McKinley, in Alaska, is the highest peak in North America.

Greenland is the world's largest island. The musk ox that live there have long, shaggy hair to protect them from the cold.

Canada's coastline is 150,933 miles (243,000 km) long—the longest in the world. This includes the country's 52,455 islands.

Lake Superior is one of the Great Lakes. It is the largest freshwater lake in the world.

Yellowstone National Park in the United States has many geysers.

This geyser is called Old Faithful because it erupts so regularly.

Spider monkeys live high up in the trees of the rain forests in Central America.

ARCTIC OCEAN

Greenland (DENMARK)

Alaska (U.S.A.)

ATLANTIC OCEAN

Hudson Bay

CANADA

ROCKY MOUNTAINS

Toronto

Great Lakes

ATLANTIC OCEAN

Great Salt Lake

Yellowstone

Great Plains

UNITED STATES

PACIFIC OCEAN

Hawaii (U.S.A.)

BAHAMAS

MEXICO

Gulf of Mexico

CUBA

DOMINICAN RPUBLIC

Mexico City

JAMAICA

HAITI

BELIZE

HONDURAS

CARIBBEAN SEA

GUATEMALA

NICARAGUA

EL SALVADOR

COSTA RICA

PANAMA

COLOMBIA

PACIFIC OCEAN

Canada geese are a common bird throughout North America. In cold weather, they travel thousands of miles (kms) south to warmer climates. They usually fly in a V formation.

With 8,705,100 people, Mexico City, Mexico, is the largest city in North America.

The library at the University of Mexico is decorated with a mural of about 7,500,000 stones.

The Caribbean Islands of North America are a favorite tourist destination. The islands have beautiful sandy beaches.

Some of the richest soil in the world can be found in the Great Plains of North America. Much of the world's wheat and corn are grown on these plains.

The SkyDome, in Toronto, Canada, is the world's first stadium with a fully retractable roof.

The Rocky Mountains run almost the entire length of western North America. People from all over the world travel to ski the Rockies.

The CN Tower in Toronto, Canada, is the highest freestanding structure in the world.

Continent	Area sq mi (sq km)	Population	Number of Countries
North America	9,400,000 (24,346,000)	501,500,000	23

United States of America

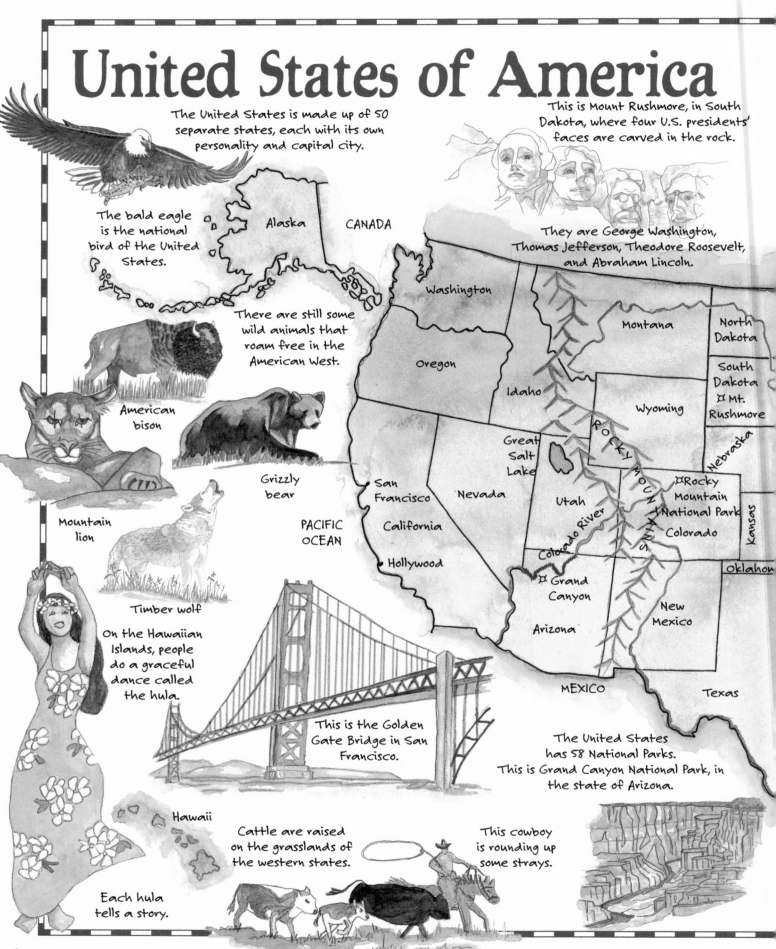

The United States is made up of 50 separate states, each with its own personality and capital city.

This is Mount Rushmore, in South Dakota, where four U.S. presidents' faces are carved in the rock.

The bald eagle is the national bird of the United States.

They are George Washington, Thomas Jefferson, Theodore Roosevelt, and Abraham Lincoln.

There are still some wild animals that roam free in the American West.

American bison

Grizzly bear

Mountain lion

Timber wolf

On the Hawaiian Islands, people do a graceful dance called the hula.

This is the Golden Gate Bridge in San Francisco.

The United States has 58 National Parks. This is Grand Canyon National Park, in the state of Arizona.

Cattle are raised on the grasslands of the western states.

This cowboy is rounding up some strays.

Each hula tells a story.

Alaska · CANADA · Washington · Oregon · Idaho · Montana · North Dakota · South Dakota · ¤ Mt. Rushmore · Wyoming · Nebraska · Great Salt Lake · ROCKY MOUNTAINS · ¤ Rocky Mountain National Park · Kansas · San Francisco · Nevada · Utah · Colorado River · Colorado · California · Hollywood · ¤ Grand Canyon · Arizona · New Mexico · Oklahoma · PACIFIC OCEAN · MEXICO · Texas · Hawaii

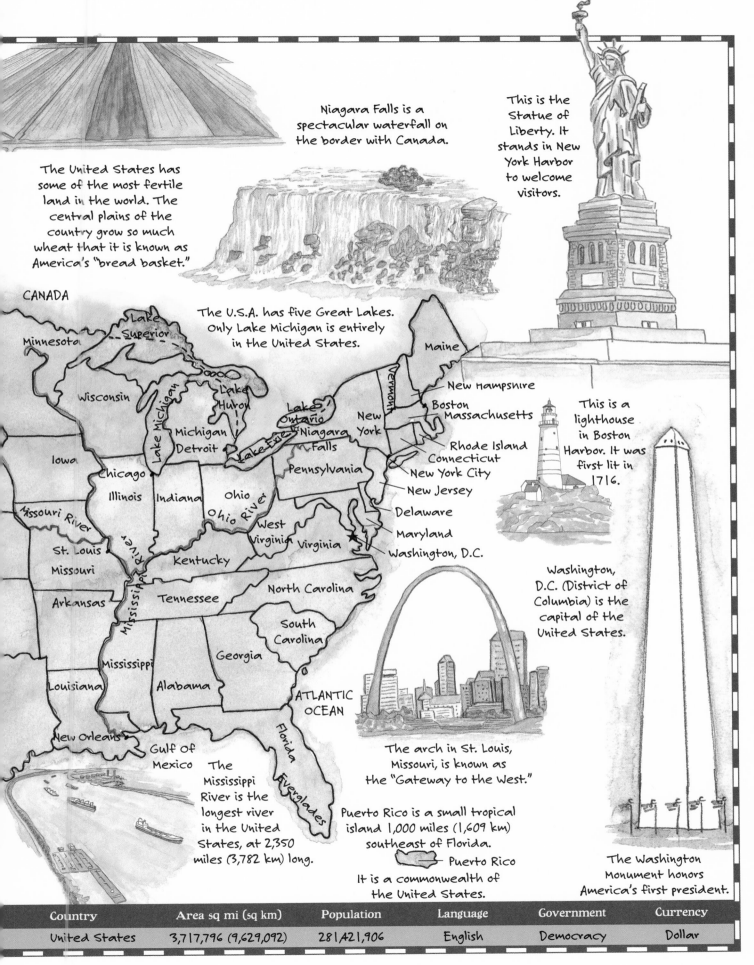

Niagara Falls is a spectacular waterfall on the border with Canada.

This is the Statue of Liberty. It stands in New York Harbor to welcome visitors.

The United States has some of the most fertile land in the world. The central plains of the country grow so much wheat that it is known as America's "bread basket."

CANADA

The U.S.A. has five Great Lakes. Only Lake Michigan is entirely in the United States.

Minnesota
Lake Superior
Wisconsin
Lake Michigan
Lake Huron
Michigan
Detroit
Lake Ontario
Lake Erie
Niagara Falls
Maine
Vermont
New Hampshire
Boston
Massachusetts
New York
Rhode Island
Connecticut
New York City
New Jersey
Delaware
Maryland
Washington, D.C.
Iowa
Chicago
Illinois
Indiana
Ohio
Ohio River
Pennsylvania
West Virginia
Virginia
Missouri River
St. Louis
Missouri
Kentucky
Arkansas
Tennessee
North Carolina
Mississippi River
South Carolina
Georgia
Mississippi
Alabama
Louisiana
New Orleans
Gulf of Mexico
Florida
Everglades
ATLANTIC OCEAN

This is a lighthouse in Boston Harbor. It was first lit in 1716.

Washington, D.C. (District of Columbia) is the capital of the United States.

The arch in St. Louis, Missouri, is known as the "Gateway to the West."

The Mississippi River is the longest river in the United States, at 2,350 miles (3,782 km) long.

Puerto Rico is a small tropical island 1,000 miles (1,609 km) southeast of Florida.

Puerto Rico

It is a commonwealth of the United States.

The Washington Monument honors America's first president.

Country	Area sq mi (sq km)	Population	Language	Government	Currency
United States	3,717,796 (9,629,092)	281,421,906	English	Democracy	Dollar

United States of America

Native Americans were the first people to settle in what is now the United States.

This Sioux boy is doing a traditional dance at a powwow in Arkansas.

In the United States, Thanksgiving is an important holiday.

Family and friends come together for a celebratory feast where turkey and special foods are often served for dinner.

Wild turkeys are found only in North America. Female turkeys are called hens. Males are toms.

Jazz music began in the United States. New Orleans, Louisiana, is known as the birthplace of jazz music.

The United States has many industries. Cars are manufactured in Detroit, Michigan.

Many American children ride a yellow school bus to school.

The Florida Everglades is one of the largest swamp areas in the world. Alligators live in the Everglades.

Roasting marshmallows over a campfire is a popular American treat on a camping trip.

Baseball is a popular sport in the United States. It is called the national pastime.

The United States has many cities with skyscrapers. This is the Sears Tower Building in Chicago, Illinois. It is one of the tallest buildings in the world.

HOLLYWOOD

Hollywood, California, is known as the movie capital of the world.

Lobsters from Maine are enjoyed around the world.

These elk are in Rocky Mountain National Park in Colorado.

Blue jeans were first made for the American farmer to wear while working. Now, they are popular all over the world.

The United States is known as a "melting pot." People of many races and cultures live there.

The Great Salt Lake in Utah is much saltier than the ocean.

The United Nations was created to bring the countries of the world together to work for peace.

Every summer, many Americans enjoy visiting state fairs. There are baking contests, animals, games, and rides.

The United Nations headquarters is located in New York City.

TICKETS

9

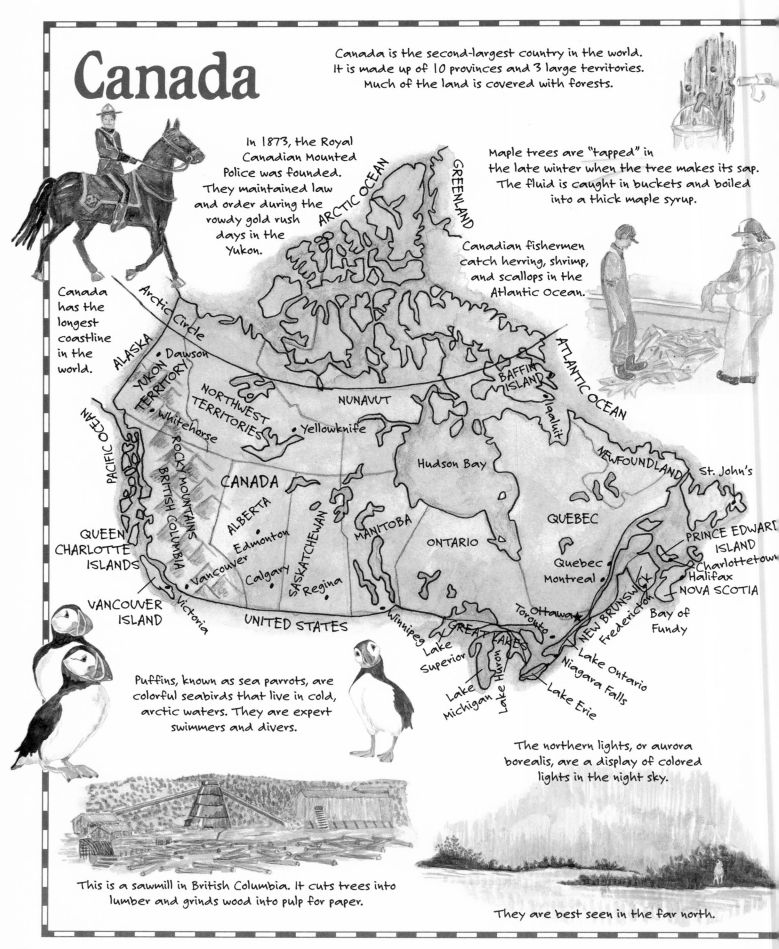

Canada

Canada is the second-largest country in the world. It is made up of 10 provinces and 3 large territories. Much of the land is covered with forests.

In 1873, the Royal Canadian Mounted Police was founded. They maintained law and order during the rowdy gold rush days in the Yukon.

Maple trees are "tapped" in the late winter when the tree makes its sap. The fluid is caught in buckets and boiled into a thick maple syrup.

Canada has the longest coastline in the world.

Canadian fishermen catch herring, shrimp, and scallops in the Atlantic Ocean.

Puffins, known as sea parrots, are colorful seabirds that live in cold, arctic waters. They are expert swimmers and divers.

The northern lights, or aurora borealis, are a display of colored lights in the night sky.

This is a sawmill in British Columbia. It cuts trees into lumber and grinds wood into pulp for paper.

They are best seen in the far north.

Map labels

ARCTIC OCEAN
GREENLAND
Arctic Circle
ALASKA
Dawson
YUKON TERRITORY
Whitehorse
NORTHWEST TERRITORIES
Yellowknife
NUNAVUT
BAFFIN ISLAND
Iqaluit
ATLANTIC OCEAN
PACIFIC OCEAN
ROCKY MOUNTAINS
BRITISH COLUMBIA
CANADA
ALBERTA
Edmonton
Hudson Bay
NEWFOUNDLAND
St. John's
QUEEN CHARLOTTE ISLANDS
Vancouver
Calgary
SASKATCHEWAN
Regina
MANITOBA
ONTARIO
QUEBEC
Quebec
Montreal
PRINCE EDWARD ISLAND
Charlottetown
Halifax
NOVA SCOTIA
VANCOUVER ISLAND
Victoria
UNITED STATES
Winnipeg
Lake Superior
GREAT LAKES
Lake Huron
Ottawa
Toronto
NEW BRUNSWICK
Fredericton
Bay of Fundy
Lake Michigan
Lake Erie
Niagara Falls
Lake Ontario

Voyageurs were French trappers in the late 1600s who traveled the Canadian waterways carrying fur to the East Coast. There are still many French-speakers in the province of Quebec.

Ice hockey is Canada's most popular sport, both to play and to watch.

Niagara Falls is actually two falls: the American Falls and Horseshoe Falls. They are a part of the border between the United States and Canada.

The curved Horseshoe Falls are on the Canadian side of the Niagara River.

The rugged Bay of Fundy has the highest tides in the world, rising up to 70 feet (21 m) daily.

The *Maid of the Mist* is a boat that takes tourists to the edge of the thundering bottom of Horseshoe Falls. Everyone wears a raincoat.

Native people of the Pacific coast are famous for their wood carvings and totem poles.

Musk ox live in the cold northern Canadian territories. The summer there is so short that the ice under the surface never fully thaws. The ground is called permafrost.

In the Arctic, some animals have brown fur that turns white in winter. When it snows, predators have a hard time seeing them because they are so white.

The Arctic Fox

Weasel

Rabbit

Country	Area sq mi (sq km)	Population	Language	Government	Currency
Canada	3,851,800 (9,976,162)	32,805,041	English/French	Parliamentary Democracy	Canadian Dollar

Mexico

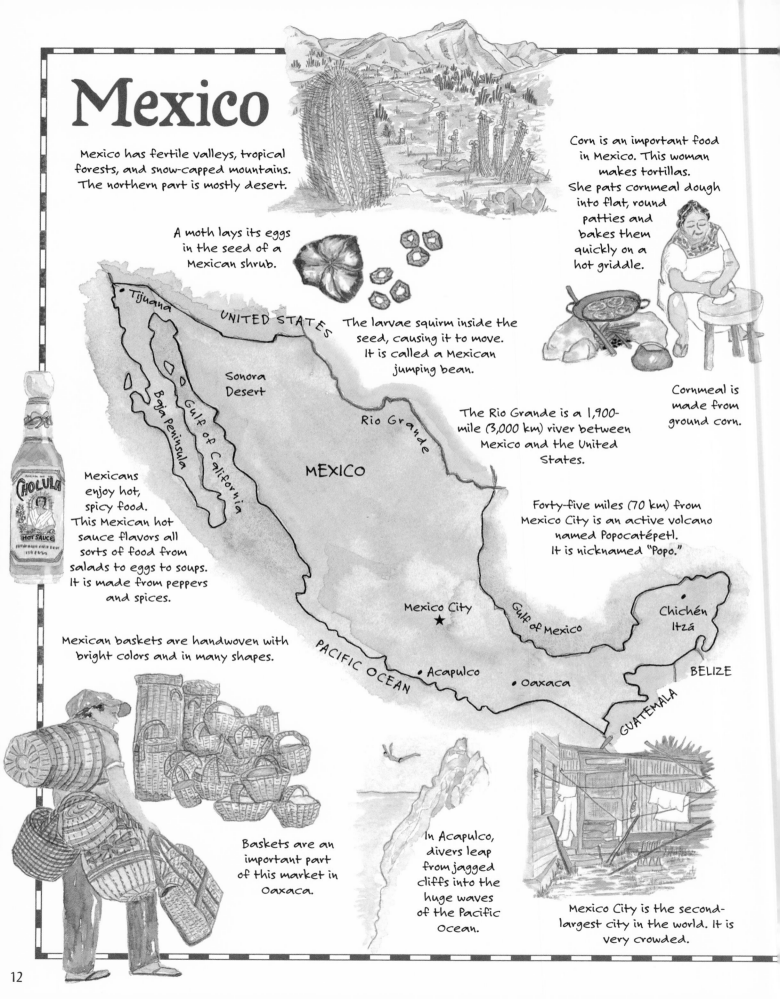

Mexico has fertile valleys, tropical forests, and snow-capped mountains. The northern part is mostly desert.

A moth lays its eggs in the seed of a Mexican shrub.

The larvae squirm inside the seed, causing it to move. It is called a Mexican jumping bean.

Corn is an important food in Mexico. This woman makes tortillas. She pats cornmeal dough into flat, round patties and bakes them quickly on a hot griddle.

Cornmeal is made from ground corn.

The Rio Grande is a 1,900-mile (3,000 km) river between Mexico and the United States.

Forty-five miles (70 km) from Mexico City is an active volcano named Popocatépetl. It is nicknamed "Popo."

Mexicans enjoy hot, spicy food. This Mexican hot sauce flavors all sorts of food from salads to eggs to soups. It is made from peppers and spices.

CHOLULA
HOT SAUCE

Mexican baskets are handwoven with bright colors and in many shapes.

Baskets are an important part of this market in Oaxaca.

In Acapulco, divers leap from jagged cliffs into the huge waves of the Pacific Ocean.

Mexico City is the second-largest city in the world. It is very crowded.

Map labels:
Tijuana
UNITED STATES
Sonora Desert
Baja Peninsula
Gulf of California
Rio Grande
MEXICO
Mexico City
Gulf of Mexico
Chichén Itzá
Acapulco
Oaxaca
PACIFIC OCEAN
GUATEMALA
BELIZE

Mariachi bands play music for dancing. The band usually includes a violin, a guitar, and a trumpet.

The quetzal bird lives in the rain forest of Mexico.

Monarch butterflies fly south to spend the winter in Mexico. Some travel up to 2,000 miles (3,200 km) from the East Coast of the United States.

Mexico was home to two major ancient civilizations: the Mayas and the Aztecs. Both built pyramids, grew corn, and had a 365-day calendar.

This is the Pyramid of Kukulcan in the ancient Mayan city of Chichén Itzá.

Mexico is the leading silver producer in the world. This silver bracelet was made in Mexico.

A piñata is a decorated papier-mâché canister filled with sugarcane, candy, peanuts, and fruit. Star piñatas are often part of Mexican celebrations. Children take turns trying to break the piñata with a stick, and then quickly gather up the scattered treats.

Fishing is an important source of food and money in Mexico. This boat is bringing in a large catch of shrimp.

Country	Area sq mi (sq km)	Population	Language	Government	Currency
Mexico	756,066 (1,958,201)	100,294,036	Spanish	Federal Republic	Peso

Central America

Belize • Costa Rica • El Salvador • Guatemala Honduras • Nicaragua • Panama

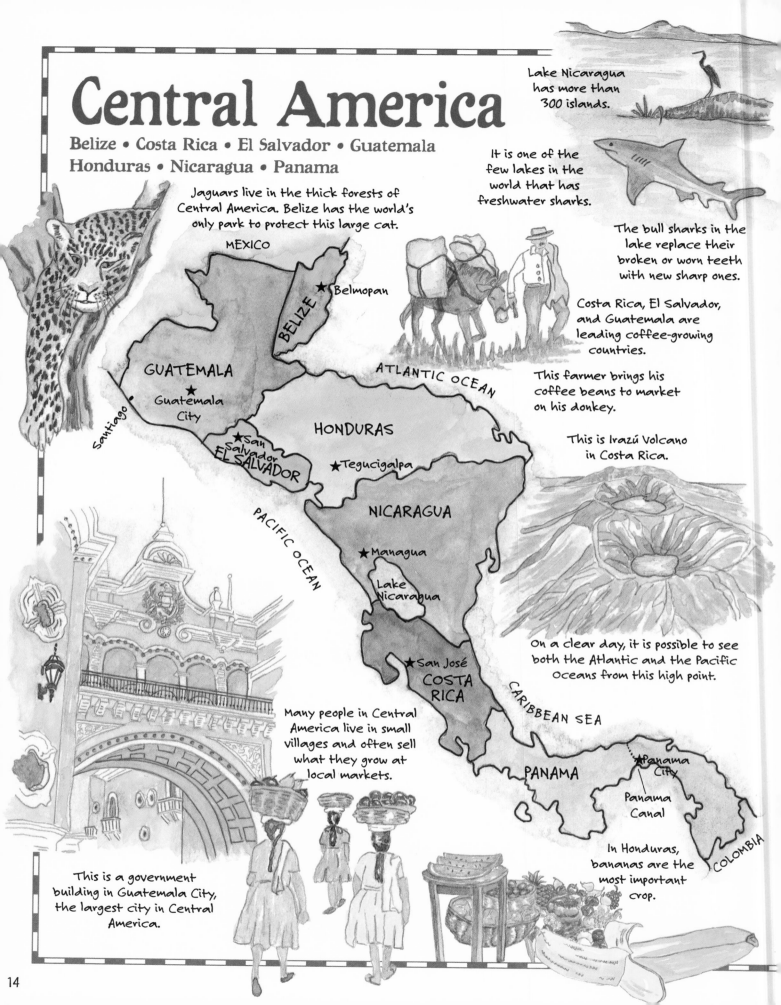

Lake Nicaragua has more than 300 islands.

It is one of the few lakes in the world that has freshwater sharks.

The bull sharks in the lake replace their broken or worn teeth with new sharp ones.

Jaguars live in the thick forests of Central America. Belize has the world's only park to protect this large cat.

Costa Rica, El Salvador, and Guatemala are leading coffee-growing countries.

This farmer brings his coffee beans to market on his donkey.

This is Irazú Volcano in Costa Rica.

On a clear day, it is possible to see both the Atlantic and the Pacific Oceans from this high point.

Many people in Central America live in small villages and often sell what they grow at local markets.

This is a government building in Guatemala City, the largest city in Central America.

In Honduras, bananas are the most important crop.

MEXICO

BELIZE — Belmopan

GUATEMALA — ★ Guatemala City

Santiago

San Salvador ★ EL SALVADOR

HONDURAS — ★ Tegucigalpa

ATLANTIC OCEAN

PACIFIC OCEAN

NICARAGUA — ★ Managua

Lake Nicaragua

★ San José COSTA RICA

CARIBBEAN SEA

PANAMA — ★ Panama City — Panama Canal

COLOMBIA

El Salvador is known as the "Land of Volcanoes." Five volcanoes appear on El Salvador's flag.

The toucan is the national bird of Belize.

A toucan's bill comes in a variety of colors.

The marimba is a percussion instrument often played in Guatemala. It makes a rich, mellow sound.

The Panama Canal is a 40-mile (64 km) man-made waterway that crosses Central America.

Every fall, the village of Santiago, Guatemala, has a kite festival.

Some kites weigh more than 200 pounds (91 kg).

It connects the Atlantic and the Pacific Oceans.

The Panama Canal has deep locks that raise and lower ships from one water level to another.

Pupusas are small cornmeal cakes stuffed with meat, beans, and spices.

Pupusas are often sold from street stands. They make a good afternoon snack.

This man from El Salvador weaves baskets and hats to sell at market.

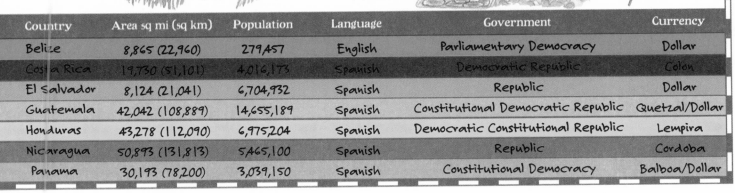

Country	Area sq mi (sq km)	Population	Language	Government	Currency
Belize	8,865 (22,960)	279,457	English	Parliamentary Democracy	Dollar
Costa Rica	19,730 (51,101)	4,016,173	Spanish	Democratic Republic	Colón
El Salvador	8,124 (21,041)	6,704,932	Spanish	Republic	Dollar
Guatemala	42,042 (108,889)	14,655,189	Spanish	Constitutional Democratic Republic	Quetzal/Dollar
Honduras	43,278 (112,090)	6,975,204	Spanish	Democratic Constitutional Republic	Lempira
Nicaragua	50,893 (131,813)	5,465,100	Spanish	Republic	Cordoba
Panama	30,193 (78,200)	3,039,150	Spanish	Constitutional Democracy	Balboa/Dollar

Caribbean Islands

Antigua and Barbuda • Bahamas
Barbados • Cuba • Dominica • Dominican
Republic Grenada • Haiti • Jamaica
St. Kitts-Nevis • St. Lucia • St. Vincent and
the Grenadines • Trinidad and Tobago

Dominicans like music with a strong beat. These are gourds filled with seeds, called maracas.

A windsurfing competition is held every year on Barbados.

This is the Cathedral San Cristóbal in Havana, Cuba. The plaza in front of the cathedral is a popular gathering place and market.

The islands of St. Kitts and Nevis are only 2 miles (3 km) apart. They both have black sand beaches.

Music is an important part of the Cuban culture. These are musicians who play on the streets of Havana, the capital city.

Pitch Lake in Trinidad is a lake of tar. Most of the surface is hard enough to walk on, but things easily sink into the softer parts.

Junkanoo is an annual parade in the Bahamas. It has colorful costumes, cowbells, whistles, and drums.

Breadfruit is common on the islands. It is a starchy, green food. This breadfruit is being roasted.

Map labels:

Nassau

BAHAMAS

ATLANTIC OCEAN

Havana

CUBA

ATLANTIC OCEAN

HAITI

Port-au-Prince

JAMAICA

Kingston

DOMINICAN REPUBLIC

Santo Domingo

Virgin Islands (USA & UK)

Turks and Caicos Islands (UK)

San Juan

Puerto Rico (USA)

Montserrat (UK)

Basseterre

ST. KITTS-NEVIS

ANTIGUA AND BARBUDA

St. John's

Guadeloupe (FRANCE)

DOMINICA

Roseau

Martinique (FRANCE)

Castries

ST. LUCIA

ST. VINCENT AND THE GRENADINES

Kingstown

BARBADOS

Bridgetown

GRENADA

St. George's

TRINIDAD AND TOBAGO

Port of Spain

VENEZUELA

Large cruise ships bring tourists from all over the world to the Caribbean Islands.

Nutmeg is an important crop in Grenada. The nutmeg fruit splits open as it ripens. The nutmeg seed is inside.

Jamaica invented a rhythmic music called reggae. The words to reggae music are in an island language known as patois.

The Trinidad and Tobago Carnival is an elaborate spring festival that lasts two days.

The smallest bird in the world is the bee hummingbird from Cuba. It is only 2 inches (5 cm) long.

Carnival is a yearly celebration with parades, colorful costumes, dancing in the streets, and a kind of folk music called calypso.

Taptaps are painted buses used in Port-au-Prince, the capital of Haiti.

There are crocodiles in the Caribbean. A croc has a narrower snout (nose) than an alligator.

Country	Area sq mi (sq km)	Population	Language	Government	Currency
Antigua and Barbuda	170 (440)	68,772	English	Constitutional Monarchy	E Car Dollar
Bahamas	5,382 (13,939)	301,790	English	Const. Parliamentary Democracy	Dollar
Barbados	166 (430)	279,254	English	Parliamentary Democracy	Dollar
Cuba	42,803 (110,860)	11,346,670	Spanish	Communist State	Cuban Peso
Dominica	290 (751)	69,029	English	Parliamentary Democracy	E Car Dollar
Dominican Republic	18,815 (48,731)	8,950,034	Spanish	Representative Democracy	Peso
Grenada	131 (339)	89,502	English	Constitutional Monarchy	E Car Dollar
Haiti	10,714 (27,749)	8,121,622	Haitian Creole & French	Elected Government	Gourde
Jamaica	4,243 (10,989)	2,731,832	English	Const. Parliamentary Democracy	Dollar
St. Kitts-Nevis	104 (269)	38,958	English	Constitutional Monarchy	E Car Dollar
St. Lucia	239 (619)	166,312	English & French Creole	Parliamentary Democracy	E Car Dollar
St. Vincent and Grenadines	150 (389)	117,534	English	Parliamentary Democracy	E Car Dollar
Trinidad and Tobago	1,981 (5,131)	1,088,644	English	Parliamentary Democracy	Dollar

South America

South America is the fourth-largest continent. It is made up of 12 different countries. It is a continent with the world's longest mountain range (the Andes) and the world's largest tropical rain forest (the Amazon River Basin).

Soccer is a popular sport throughout all of South America.

The mighty Amazon River is the second-longest river in the world. In some places, the Amazon is too wide to see across.

PANAMA

VENEZUELA
★ Caracas
¤ Angel Falls

Georgetown
SURINAME
Paramaribo
Cayenne
★ Bogotá
French Guiana
COLOMBIA
GUYANA
(FRANCE)

Equator
ATLANTIC OCEAN

Galápagos Islands (ECUADOR)
★ Quito
ECUADOR

Amazon River
Amazon River Basin

This is Aconcagua, the highest point in South America.

PERU

BRAZIL

Lima ★

Nazca ¤
Lake Titicaca
★ Brasília

BOLIVIA
★ Sucre

PACIFIC OCEAN

ANDES MOUNTAINS

CHILE

PARAGUAY
★ Asunción

ATLANTIC OCEAN

This is a park in Buenos Aires.

Aconcagua
▲ 22,831 ft.
(6,959 m)

¤ Iguaçú Falls

Patagonia is an area in the south of the continent that is in both Argentina and Chile. The name comes from the Spanish word that means "Big Feet," because the early natives wore boots stuffed with straw for warmth.

URUGUAY

Buenos Aires ★
Montevideo

Santiago ★
ARGENTINA

One out of every three people in Argentina lives in Buenos Aires, the capital.

Cape Horn

The Paine Towers are beautiful craggy mountains. They are found in the southern tip of Chile.

Brazil and Ecuador produce most of the world's bananas. Bananas are picked green and ripen on their way to market because they lose their flavor if they become yellow on the plant.

More than 2,000 years ago, 300 line drawings were etched in the desert by the Nazca people of Peru.

This Nazca drawing is of a bird.

The drawings are so large that most are best seen from the air.

There is a network of high mountain footpaths in the Andes Mountains called the Inca Trail.

Tunnels are carved through the rock.

Stone steps go up and over passes. Bridges made of ropes stretch across roaring rivers.

Bamboo panpipes are a traditional musical instrument heard throughout the Andes Mountains.

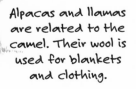

Alpacas and llamas are related to the camel. Their wool is used for blankets and clothing.

In 1937, an American pilot named Jimmy Angel spotted these falls from the air when he was searching for gold in the area. Angel Falls in Venezuela is the world's highest waterfall.

Continent	Area sq mi (sq km)	Population	Number of Countries
South America	6,900,000 (17,871,000)	379,500,000	12

North Andean South America

Colombia • Ecuador • Peru • Venezuela

The Andes Mountains are the world's longest mountain range above sea level. They stretch along the entire west coast of South America.

Panama hats are so flexible that they can be rolled up.

Ecuador's Cotopaxi is one of the highest active volcanoes in the world. It has erupted 50 times in the past 400 years.

Surprisingly, Panama hats are woven in Ecuador. Their name comes from the Panama Canal builders who wore them to block the sun.

The Orinoco River in Venezuela is so shallow in places that only the smallest boats can get through. *Orinoco* means "a place to paddle."

Colombia is well known for growing flavorful coffee. Coffee trees have white blossoms with red berries.

The people in North Andean countries weave brightly colored materials and wear ponchos to keep themselves warm.

Coffee beans are dried in the sun and then roasted to bring out the flavor.

ATLANTIC OCEAN

★ Caracas

VENEZUELA

Orinoco River

GUYANA

PANAMA

Cauca River

PACIFIC OCEAN

★ Bogotá

COLOMBIA

BRAZIL

Galápagos Islands

★ Quito

ECUADOR

PERU

ANDES MOUNTAINS

PACIFIC OCEAN

★ Lima

BOLIVIA

Lake Titicaca

CHILE

In the 1400s, the Incas built a large empire in the Andes Mountains of Peru.

These are the ruins of Machu Picchu, an Incan city.

Potatoes were first grown in Peru. They have up to 3,000 kinds of potatoes—even freeze-dried.

The great stone structures the Incas built were so tightly constructed that a blade of grass could not fit between the stones.

The Galápagos Islands in the Pacific Ocean belong to Ecuador. Ecuador has the largest variety of plants and animals in the world.

Marine iguanas on the Galápagos collect salt in their noses when feeding underwater.

The salt is sneezed up into the air and falls back on their heads, leaving white deposits.

Sally lightfoot crabs vary in color from island to island.

Galápagos tortoises live longer than any other creature on Earth—up to 150 years.

Country	Area sq mi (sq km)	Population	Language	Government	Currency
Colombia	440,762 (1,141,574)	42,954,279	Spanish	Republic	Peso
Ecuador	105,037 (272,046)	13,363,593	Spanish	Republic	U.S. Dollar
Peru	496,223 (1,285,218)	27,925,628	Spanish	Constitutional Republic	New Sol
Venezuela	352,143 (912,054)	25,375,281	Spanish	Federal Republic	Bolivar

Eastern South America

Brazil • Guyana • Suriname

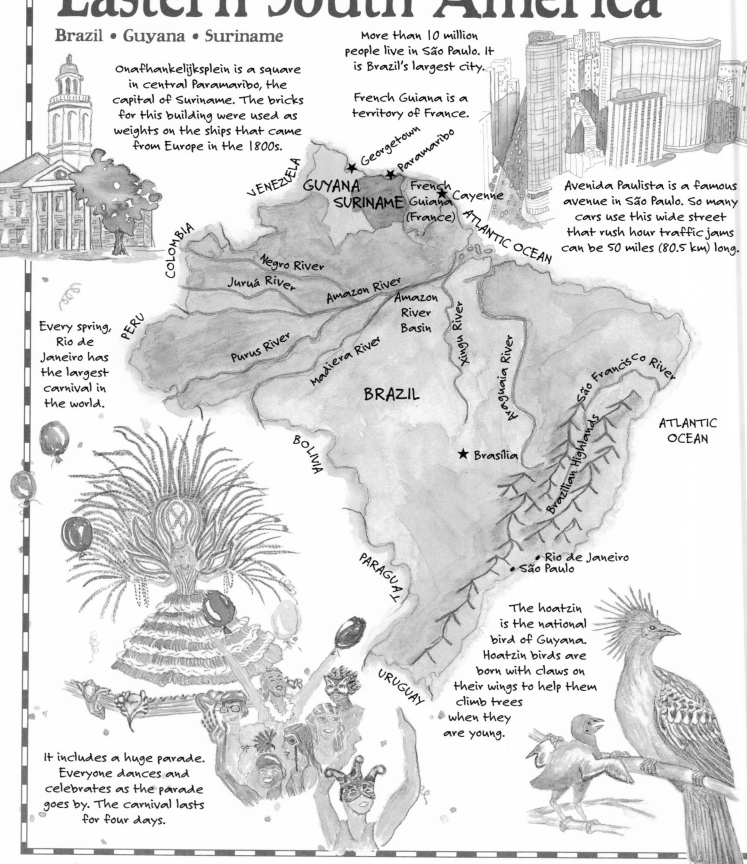

Onafhankelijksplein is a square in central Paramaribo, the capital of Suriname. The bricks for this building were used as weights on the ships that came from Europe in the 1800s.

More than 10 million people live in São Paulo. It is Brazil's largest city.

French Guiana is a territory of France.

Avenida Paulista is a famous avenue in São Paulo. So many cars use this wide street that rush hour traffic jams can be 50 miles (80.5 km) long.

Every spring, Rio de Janeiro has the largest carnival in the world.

It includes a huge parade. Everyone dances and celebrates as the parade goes by. The carnival lasts for four days.

The hoatzin is the national bird of Guyana. Hoatzin birds are born with claws on their wings to help them climb trees when they are young.

VENEZUELA
Georgetown
Paramaribo
GUYANA
SURINAME
French Guiana (France)
★ Cayenne
COLOMBIA
ATLANTIC OCEAN
Negro River
Juruá River
Amazon River
Amazon River Basin
PERU
Purus River
Madiera River
Xingu River
Araguaia River
São Francisco River
Brazilian Highlands
BRAZIL
BOLIVIA
★ Brasília
ATLANTIC OCEAN
PARAGUAY
• Rio de Janeiro
• São Paulo
URUGUAY

The Amazon River Basin in Brazil has the largest rain forest in the world.

Macaws often fly in pairs above the forest.

Boa constrictor snakes can grow up to 14 feet (4.3 m) long.

Cayenne peppers, known as "red hots," originally came from Cayenne, the capital of French Guiana.

In 1958, when the famous soccer player Pelé was only 17, he helped Brazil win a World Cup victory. In his career, he made 1,283 goals playing what he called a "beautiful game." Pelé led his team on to win a total of three World Cups.

In the Amazon jungle, this howler monkey's call can be heard up to 3 miles (4.8 km) away in open areas.

Logging, farming, and mining are destroying much of the rain forest. Once a rain forest is destroyed, it is gone forever!

The blue poison arrow frog lives in Suriname. Natives poison their arrows for hunting by wiping them over the frog's skin.

On some street corners in Brazil, women in white dresses sell acaraj, fried beans wrapped around meat or seafood.

Country	Area sq mi (sq km)	Population	Language	Government	Currency
Brazil	3,286,470 (8,511,957)	186,112,794	Portuguese	Federative Republic	Real
Guyana	83,000 (214,970)	765,283	English/Creole	Republic	Dollar
Suriname	63,039 (163,272)	438,144	Dutch	Constitutional Democracy	Dollar

South Andean South America

Argentina • Bolivia • Chile
Paraguay • Uruguay

Argentina comes from the Latin word *Argentum*, which means "silver." Gold, silver, zinc, and copper are still mined in many South American countries.

In Paraguay, the women make a fine lace called nanduti, which means "spiderweb."

Lake Titicaca is the highest navigable lake in the world that ships can sail on. It is on the border of Peru and Bolivia.

Maté is a popular hot tea made with yerba maté leaves from the rain forest. The tea is sucked through a straw, which filters out the leaves.

Reeds grow on the banks of the lake. Villagers use the reeds to make boats called totoras.

Cape Horn is at the southern tip of Chile. Sailors dread going "around the horn" because of its stormy waters and high waves.

Map labels:

PERU
Lake Titicaca
★ La Paz
BOLIVIA
★ Sucre
BRAZIL
PARAGUAY
Asunción ★
Atacama Desert
PACIFIC OCEAN
CHILE
ANDES MOUNTAINS
ARGENTINA
¤ Iguaçú Falls
URUGUAY
★ Montevideo
Buenos Aires ★
ATLANTIC OCEAN
★ Santiago
Cape Horn

Avenida 9 de Julio (Avenue of July 9) in Buenos Aires, Argentina, is the world's widest boulevard. It has 16 lanes. July 9 is Argentina's independence day.

The English brought polo to Argentina. Polo is similar to field hockey but is played on horseback.

Argentina has dominated the sport for many years.

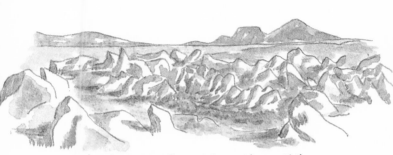

The Atacama Desert in northern Chile averages less than half an inch (1.27 cm) of rain per year!

Cowboys in Argentina and Uruguay are called gauchos. Gauchos ride horses and herd cattle.

The tango is a popular dance in Argentina. It is a very difficult and dramatic dance.

Gauchos wear ponchos for warmth and to protect themselves from the sun.

Dancing the tango

The spectacular Iguaçú Falls are found on the border of Argentina and Brazil. The falls are over 2 miles (3.2 km) wide and fall more than 200 feet (61 m).

Argentina is one of the world's biggest producers of beef. Beef from Argentina is said to be some of the best in the world.

Country	Area sq mi (sq km)	Population	Language	Government	Currency
Argentina	1,072,156 (2,738,972)	39,537,943	Spanish	Republic	Peso
Bolivia	424,162 (1,098,580)	8,857,870	Spanish/Quechua/Aymara	Republic	Boliviano
Chile	292,258 (756,948)	15,980,912	Spanish	Republic	Peso
Paraguay	157,046 (406,749)	6,347,884	Spanish/Guaraní	Constitutional Republic	Guaraní
Uruguay	68,039 (176,221)	3,415,920	Spanish	Constitutional Republic	Peso

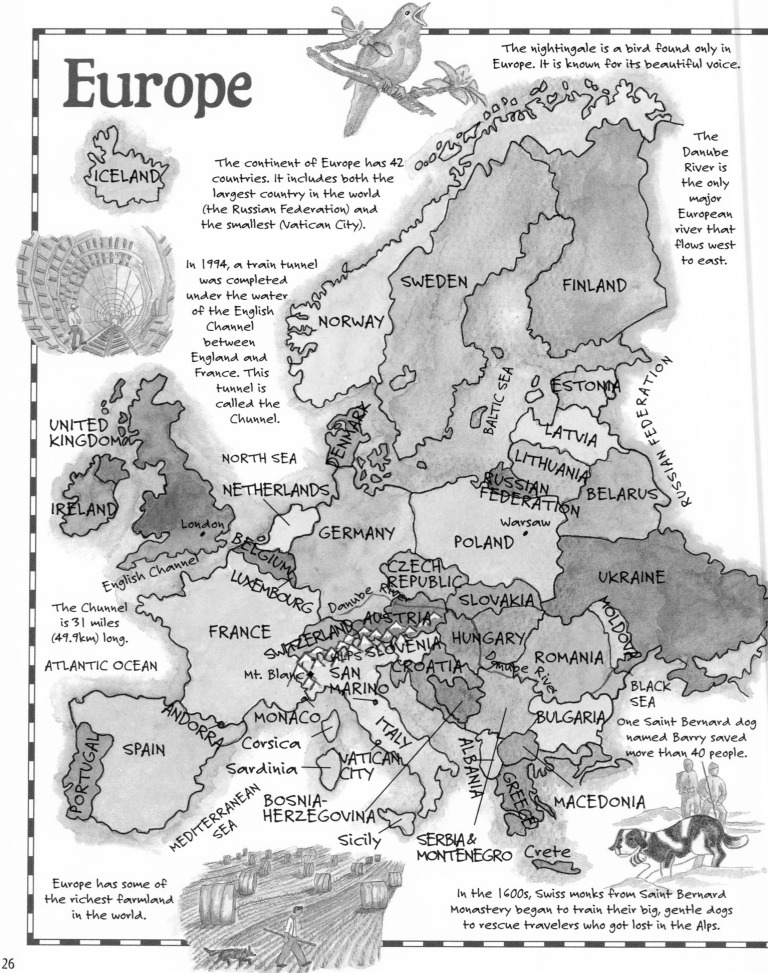

Europe

The nightingale is a bird found only in Europe. It is known for its beautiful voice.

ICELAND

The continent of Europe has 42 countries. It includes both the largest country in the world (the Russian Federation) and the smallest (Vatican City).

The Danube River is the only major European river that flows west to east.

In 1994, a train tunnel was completed under the water of the English Channel between England and France. This tunnel is called the Chunnel.

SWEDEN

NORWAY

FINLAND

BALTIC SEA

ESTONIA

LATVIA

LITHUANIA

RUSSIAN FEDERATION

UNITED KINGDOM

NORTH SEA

DENMARK

NETHERLANDS

London

BELGIUM

GERMANY

POLAND

Warsaw

BELARUS

IRELAND

English Channel

The Chunnel is 31 miles (49.9km) long.

ATLANTIC OCEAN

LUXEMBOURG

CZECH REPUBLIC

Danube River

SLOVAKIA

UKRAINE

FRANCE

SWITZERLAND

AUSTRIA

ALPS

SLOVENIA

HUNGARY

MOLDOVA

Mt. Blanc

SAN MARINO

CROATIA

Danube River

ROMANIA

ANDORRA

MONACO

Corsica

ITALY

VATICAN CITY

Sardinia

SPAIN

PORTUGAL

MEDITERRANEAN SEA

BOSNIA-HERZEGOVINA

Sicily

ALBANIA

GREECE

BLACK SEA

BULGARIA

MACEDONIA

SERBIA & MONTENEGRO

Crete

One Saint Bernard dog named Barry saved more than 40 people.

Europe has some of the richest farmland in the world.

In the 1600s, Swiss monks from Saint Bernard Monastery began to train their big, gentle dogs to rescue travelers who got lost in the Alps.

26

The London skyline

More people live in London than in any other European city.

Neuschwanstein, or Mad Ludwig's Castle, in Germany was built in the 1870s by King Ludwig II. It was a model for castles in the Walt Disney theme parks.

This is the front of a one-Euro coin.

San Marino

The backs of the coins are different.

Finland

Many countries in Europe have joined together as the European Union (EU). They have a common unit of money called the Euro.

The Zaluski Library

There are about 60 languages spoken in Europe.

Guten Tag
"Good day" in German

Bonjour
"Good day" in French

Buenos dias
"Good day" in Spanish

Ciao
"Good day" in Italian

The first public library in the world was built in 1747 in Warsaw, Poland.

Europe has a 750 mile (1,200 km) long mountain range called the Alps. People from all over the world come to the Alps to ski, hike, and enjoy the mountains in any weather.

These climbers are in France at the peak of a rock near Mount Blanc, the highest mountain in the Alps.

The continent of Europe has snow-covered mountains and warm, sunny beaches. It has no desert.

The Mediterranean beach in southern France is called the Riviera.

Continent	Area sq mi (sq km)	Population	Number of countries
Europe	4,000,000 (10,400,000)	542,578,000	42

Scandinavia

Denmark • Finland • Iceland Norway • Sweden

This is a Russian church in Helsinki, the capital of Finland. Finland has been greatly influenced by its neighbor, the Russian Federation.

Fishing is important to this region for both food and money.

This man has drilled a hole in the ice to catch his dinner.

The Sámi dress in colorful, warm clothes. They often raise reindeer.

Reykjavik, the capital of Iceland, is known for its brightly colored rooftops.

Sámi live in the most northern parts of Norway, Sweden, and Finland.

ICELAND
★ Reykjavik

RUSSIAN FEDERATION

ATLANTIC OCEAN

FINLAND

SWEDEN

Gulf of Bothnia

NORWAY

★ Helsinki

Dala horses like this one are made from wood and hand painted. They have become a symbol of Sweden.

★ Stockholm

Oslo ★

BALTIC SEA

DENMARK

★ Copenhagen

GERMANY

Vikings were a seafaring people from Denmark, Norway, and Sweden. They were explorers, fierce pirates, and warriors.

In winter, Swedes celebrate St. Lucia Day. Early on December 13, the eldest daughter carries light to the family by wearing a wreath of candles on her head. She brings them coffee and cakes.

The entire coast of Norway has narrow, steep bays. They are called fjords.

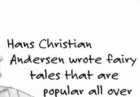

Skiing is popular in these snowy countries.

Lumber and other forest products from Finland are sold to many countries.

Tivoli Gardens is a famous amusement park in Copenhagen, Denmark. Marching bands and concerts can be heard in the park.

Smorgasbord is a buffet type meal. In Sweden, it is meant to be eaten in a certain order.

Hans Christian Andersen wrote fairy tales that are popular all over the world.

His statue is in Copenhagen, the capital of Denmark.

Thumbalina
The Brave Tin Soldier
The Ugly Duckling
The Little Mermaid

Trolls are creatures in Norwegian folklore. In stories, they often live under bridges and demand payment from people who wish to cross.

These open-faced sandwiches are served on a wooden board in Denmark.

Country	Area sq mi (sq km)	Population	Language	Government	Currency
Denmark	16,639 (43,095)	5,432,335	Danish	Constitutional Monarchy	Krone
Finland	130,559 (338,145)	5,223,442	Finnish, Swedish	Republic	Euro
Iceland	40,000 (100,000)	296,737	Icelandic	Constitutional Republic	Krona
Norway	125,050 (323,878)	4,593,041	Norwegian	Constitutional Monarchy	Krone
Sweden	173,731 (449,963)	9,001,774	Swedish	Constitutional Monarchy	Krona

British Isles
United Kingdom • Republic of Ireland

Blarney Castle

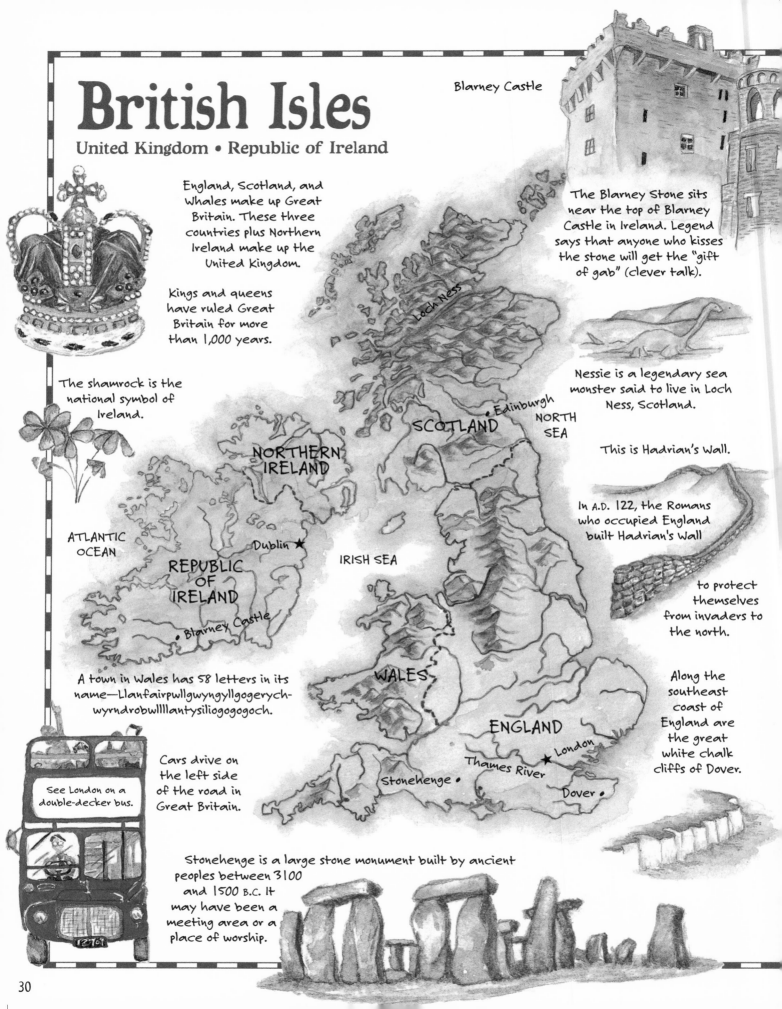

England, Scotland, and Whales make up Great Britain. These three countries plus Northern Ireland make up the United Kingdom.

Kings and queens have ruled Great Britain for more than 1,000 years.

The shamrock is the national symbol of Ireland.

The Blarney Stone sits near the top of Blarney Castle in Ireland. Legend says that anyone who kisses the stone will get the "gift of gab" (clever talk).

Nessie is a legendary sea monster said to live in Loch Ness, Scotland.

This is Hadrian's Wall.

In A.D. 122, the Romans who occupied England built Hadrian's Wall to protect themselves from invaders to the north.

Loch Ness

Edinburgh

SCOTLAND

NORTH SEA

NORTHERN IRELAND

ATLANTIC OCEAN

Dublin ★

REPUBLIC OF IRELAND

IRISH SEA

• Blarney Castle

A town in Wales has 58 letters in its name—Llanfairpwllgwyngyllgogerych-wyrndrobwllllantysiliogogogoch.

WALES

Along the southeast coast of England are the great white chalk cliffs of Dover.

ENGLAND

London ★

Thames River

Stonehenge •

Dover •

See London on a double-decker bus.

Cars drive on the left side of the road in Great Britain.

Stonehenge is a large stone monument built by ancient peoples between 3100 and 1500 B.C. It may have been a meeting area or a place of worship.

In Scotland, families are called clans. Each clan has its own plaid cloth, or tartan, often worn as a kilt.

William Shakespeare (1564-1616) is a famous English playwright and poet. He created familiar words and phrases such as bump, lonely, and catch cold.

Thistles are prickly plants that grow all over Scotland.

Piccadilly Circus, in London, is a busy plaza with a fountain. People often meet on the fountain's steps.

Traditionally, Scots enjoy bagpipe music and dancing the Highland fling.

The bell in this famous clock tower is known as "Big Ben."

The Tower Bridge crosses the Thames River. It is both a suspension bridge and a drawbridge.

The people of Great Britain like to work in their gardens and drink hot tea.

The Tower of London

The Tower of London was built as a fortress on the Thames River in 1066. It has been used as a prison, a palace, a royal mint, a vault for crown jewels, and a zoo.

Soccer, rugby, and cricket all originated in Great Britain.

The English countryside is a patchwork of hedges and sheep.

Country	Area sq mi (sq km)	Population	Language	Government	Currency
United Kingdom	94,248 (244,101)	60,441,457	English	Constitutional Monarchy	English pound
Republic of Ireland	27,136 (70,282)	4,015,676	English & Gaelic	Republic	Irish pound

Spain and Portugal

Spain and Portugal together make the Iberian Peninsula.

The Meseta is a dry plateau covering most of Spain and some of Portugal. Sheep graze in the highlands.

Olive trees grow all over the Spanish countryside. Spain produces more olive oil than any other country.

The Basques live in the foothills of the Spanish Pyrenees. Their language is unlike any other in the world.

Cork comes from the bark of the cork oak tree, which grows in many parts of Portugal and Spain.

ATLANTIC OCEAN

ATLANTIC OCEAN

• Bilbao

FRANCE

• Porto

Pamplona •

ANDORRA

PYRENEES

PORTUGAL

• Segovia

Ebro River

★ Madrid

Barcelona •

Tagus River

★ Lisbon

• Toledo

SPAIN

Guadiana River

Valencia •

Guadalquivir River

• Seville

ATLANTIC OCEAN

Gibraltar (U.K.)

• Granada

Strait of Gibraltar

MEDITERRANEAN SEA

AFRICA

Spain and Portugal have many beautiful cathedrals and religious festivals.

The Rock of Gibraltar stands at the southern tip of Spain, about 8 miles (13 km) across the water from North Africa.

Portuguese fishermen and fisherwomen brave the rugged Atlantic waters to fish in small boats. Fish is an important part of the diet in Portugal. They are also exported to other countries.

Once a year, in a small town festival near Valencia, people throw overripe tomatoes at one another.

Food is often bought in an open market. Families might gather for lunch and then take a siesta (or nap) in the heat of the day.

Castanets are two shells that dancers hold in their hands and click together in time to the music.

Paella is a favorite Spanish meal made with rice, shellfish, and vegetables.

Flamenco is a dramatic, lively type of music, often performed with a guitar, singers, and dancers.

The running of the bulls is part of a festival where people run with bulls through the streets of Pamplona.

The Alhambra is a palace and a fortress built between 1238 and 1358. It overlooks the city of Granada.

This dangerous tradition occurs every July.

Soccer is a popular sport in both Spain and Portugal.

Warm, sunny weather along the Mediterranean coast attracts people from all over the world to Spain's sandy beaches.

Country	Area sq mi (sq km)	Population	Language	Government	Currency
Portugal	35,672 (92,390)	10,566,212	Portuguese	Parliamentary Democracy	Euro
Spain	194,898 (504,783)	40,341,462	Spanish	Parliamentary Democracy	Euro

France

France • Andorra • Monaco

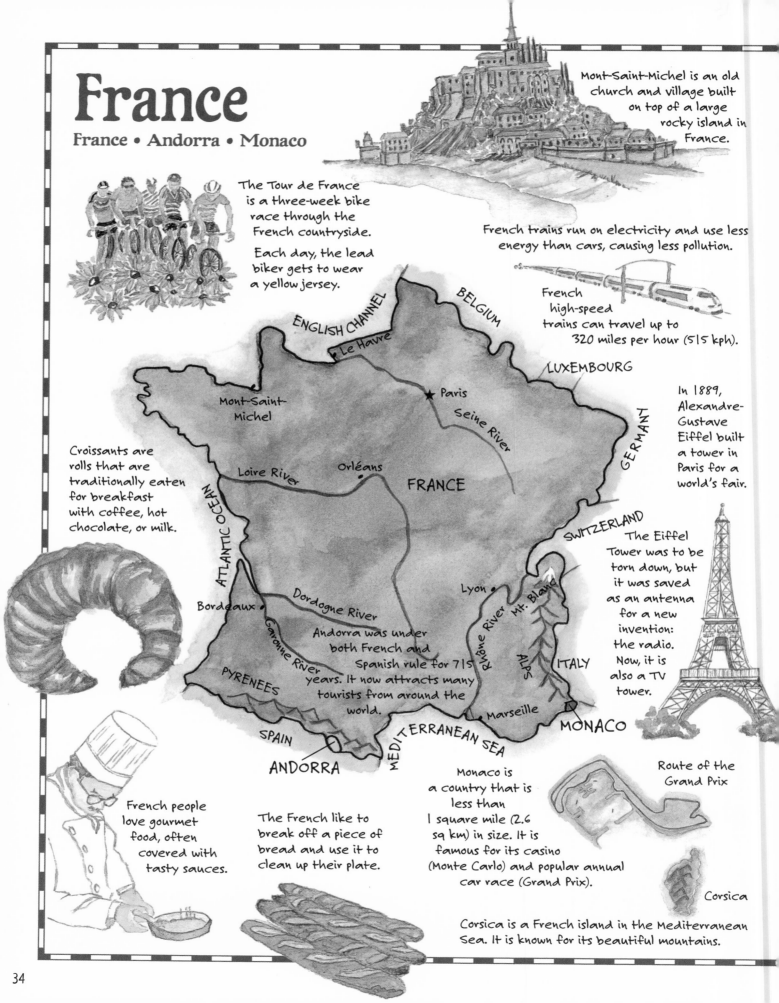

Mont-Saint-Michel is an old church and village built on top of a large rocky island in France.

The Tour de France is a three-week bike race through the French countryside.

Each day, the lead biker gets to wear a yellow jersey.

French trains run on electricity and use less energy than cars, causing less pollution.

French high-speed trains can travel up to 320 miles per hour (515 kph).

ENGLISH CHANNEL
BELGIUM
Le Havre
LUXEMBOURG
Paris
Mont-Saint-Michel
Seine River
GERMANY
Loire River
Orléans
FRANCE
ATLANTIC OCEAN
SWITZERLAND
Croissants are rolls that are traditionally eaten for breakfast with coffee, hot chocolate, or milk.

Bordeaux
Dordogne River
Lyon
Mt. Blanc
Garonne River
Rhône River
ALPS
ITALY
PYRENEES
Andorra was under both French and Spanish rule for 715 years. It now attracts many tourists from around the world.
SPAIN
MEDITERRANEAN SEA
ANDORRA
MONACO

In 1889, Alexandre-Gustave Eiffel built a tower in Paris for a world's fair.

The Eiffel Tower was to be torn down, but it was saved as an antenna for a new invention: the radio. Now, it is also a TV tower.

Marseille

Route of the Grand Prix

French people love gourmet food, often covered with tasty sauces.

The French like to break off a piece of bread and use it to clean up their plate.

Monaco is a country that is less than 1 square mile (2.6 sq km) in size. It is famous for its casino (Monte Carlo) and popular annual car race (Grand Prix).

Corsica

Corsica is a French island in the Mediterranean Sea. It is known for its beautiful mountains.

The French people make and export some of the best wine in the world.

Construction of the Cathedral of Notre-Dame began in 1163 and took more than 180 years to complete.

The center of a French village is usually an old church surrounded by small cafés and shops.

The French countryside is rich with meadows, hills, forests, vineyards, and small villages.

Seine River

The cathedral stands on an island in the Seine River in the center of Paris.

Much of the French countryside is used to raise cattle for meat and dairy products. French cheese is prized all over the world.

L'Arc de Triomphe

In 1806, Emperor Napoleon I built an enormous archway in Paris to honor his armies. L'Arc de Triomphe (the Arch of Triumph) stands at the head of a long and beautiful boulevard with shops and cafés.

Originally built as a fortress, the Louvre became a grand palace for the kings of France.

In 1984, an enormous glass pyramid was built in the Louvre's courtyard and is now the museum's entrance.

The Louvre is one of the largest, most famous art museums in the world.

Parisians and tourists like to spend long hours eating and visiting in the city's cafés.

Country	Area sq mi (sq km)	Population	Language	Government	Currency
Andorra	181 (469)	70,549	Catalan	Parliamentary Democracy	Euro
France	211,208 (547,029)	60,656,178	French	Republic	Euro
Monaco	.75 (1.95)	32,409	French	Constitutional Monarchy	Euro

Northwest Europe

Belgium • Luxembourg • Netherlands

The Netherlands is also known as Holland. The land is very low and wet.

In winter, the canals freeze and the people, known as the Dutch, like to ice skate on them.

It is constant work to keep the sea from flooding the dry land. For years, windmills pumped water back into the sea.

Belgium is famous for its handmade lace.

In the Netherlands, wooden shoes, or clogs, are traditionally worn. They are easy to get on and off, and they keep the feet dry.

This is a gray heron, a bird of the Netherlands.

NORTH SEA

Amsterdam

NETHERLANDS

The Hague

Rotterdam

GERMANY

Antwerp

Brussels

BELGIUM

The Netherlands has 12,000 miles (20,000 km) of bike paths.

FRANCE

LUXEMBOURG

Luxembourg

The heron has long legs and likes to wade in the water.

Most Dutch people ride bikes.

The Netherlands has all kinds of bridges to cross its many waterways.

This is Erasmus Bridge in the city of Rotterdam. This bridge is nicknamed "The Swan" because it looks so graceful over the water.

The Netherlands is famous for cheese.

This Edam cheese is wrapped in wax to help keep it fresh.

Brussels is the capital of Belgium.

The roofs of many old Belgian houses are shaped like steps.

This is Bourscheid Castle in Luxembourg, complete with a two-level dungeon.

Some people in Luxembourg speak a language called Letzeburgesch.

The Netherlands is famous for its tulips, daffodils, and other flowers.

Antwerp, Belgium, is a major center for diamond cutting and polishing.

In the 1840s, a Belgian musician, Adolphe Sax, invented the first saxophone.

Many great artists were Dutch, such as Rembrandt van Rijn and Johannes Vermeer.

This is a painting that Vincent van Gogh made of himself.

Belgian and Dutch chocolate is prized all over the world.

This is a Dutch chocolate layer cake.

Country	Area sq mi (sq km)	Population	Language	Government	Currency
Belgium	11,780 (30,510)	10,364,388	Dutch/French	Federal Parliamentary Democracy	Euro
Luxembourg	999 (2,587)	468,571	Luxembourgish	Constitutional Monarchy	Euro
Netherlands	16,033 (41,525)	16,407,491	Dutch	Constitutional Monarchy	Euro

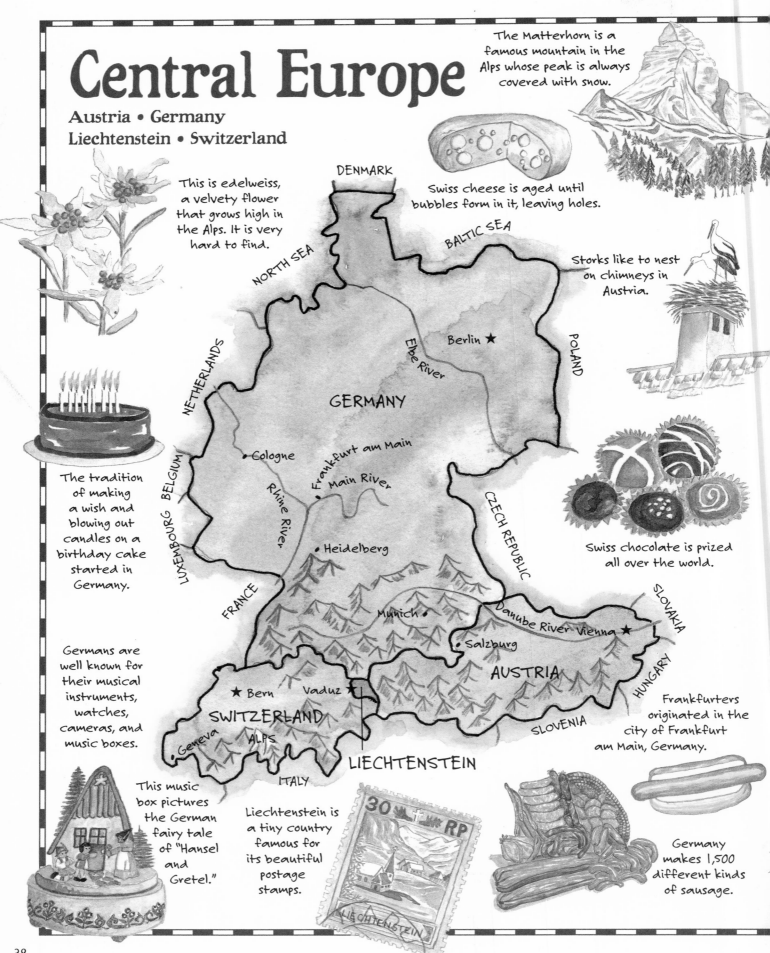

Central Europe

Austria • Germany
Liechtenstein • Switzerland

The Matterhorn is a famous mountain in the Alps whose peak is always covered with snow.

This is edelweiss, a velvety flower that grows high in the Alps. It is very hard to find.

Swiss cheese is aged until bubbles form in it, leaving holes.

Storks like to nest on chimneys in Austria.

DENMARK

NORTH SEA

BALTIC SEA

Berlin ★

Elbe River

GERMANY

POLAND

Cologne •

Frankfurt am Main

• Main River

Rhine River

CZECH REPUBLIC

Swiss chocolate is prized all over the world.

The tradition of making a wish and blowing out candles on a birthday cake started in Germany.

• Heidelberg

Germans are well known for their musical instruments, watches, cameras, and music boxes.

Munich •

Danube River Vienna ★

SLOVAKIA

• Salzburg

AUSTRIA

HUNGARY

★ Bern   Vaduz ★

SWITZERLAND

Frankfurters originated in the city of Frankfurt am Main, Germany.

SLOVENIA

• Geneva   ALPS

LIECHTENSTEIN

ITALY

This music box pictures the German fairy tale of "Hansel and Gretel."

Liechtenstein is a tiny country famous for its beautiful postage stamps.

30 RP

LIECHTENSTEIN

Germany makes 1,500 different kinds of sausage.

The first cuckoo clocks were hand carved during the long German winters.

Around 1440, a German named Johannes Gutenberg made a printing press. Books could be printed faster and cheaper, so more people began to read.

The Brandenburg Gate is a famous landmark in the German capital city of Berlin. It was finished in 1791.

Germany is home to many car companies.

Many great musicians and composers came from Austria, including Ludwig van Beethoven and Wolfgang Amadeus Mozart.

Lederhosen are short leather pants originally worn by farmers in the 1700s.

A dirndl is a dress with an apron. It was first worn by peasants.

In the Alps, people may live in a cottage called a chalet. They put rocks on the roof to protect it from strong mountain winds.

The alpenhorn is an instrument used by mountain herders to call their cows. Its sound can be heard up to 8 miles (13 km) away.

Country	Area sq mi (sq km)	Population	Language	Government	Currency
Austria	32,375 (83,851)	8,184,691	German	Federal Republic	Euro
Germany	137,828 (356,974)	82,431,390	German	Federal Republic	Euro
Liechtenstein	62 (161)	33,717	German	Hereditary Constitutional	Swiss Franc
Switzerland	15,942 (41,290)	7,489,370	Ger./French/Ital.	Federal Republic	Franc

North Central Europe

Bulgaria • Czech Republic • Hungary
Poland • Romania • Slovakia

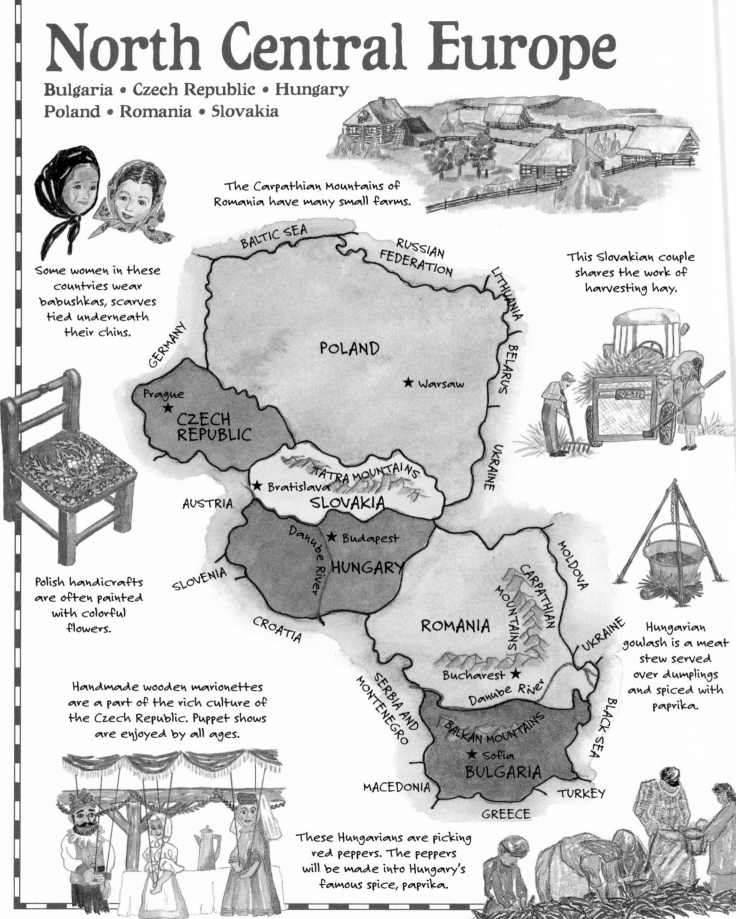

The Carpathian Mountains of Romania have many small farms.

Some women in these countries wear babushkas, scarves tied underneath their chins.

This Slovakian couple shares the work of harvesting hay.

Polish handicrafts are often painted with colorful flowers.

Handmade wooden marionettes are a part of the rich culture of the Czech Republic. Puppet shows are enjoyed by all ages.

Hungarian goulash is a meat stew served over dumplings and spiced with paprika.

These Hungarians are picking red peppers. The peppers will be made into Hungary's famous spice, paprika.

BALTIC SEA

RUSSIAN FEDERATION

LITHUANIA

BELARUS

GERMANY

POLAND

★ Warsaw

Prague
★
CZECH REPUBLIC

UKRAINE

TATRA MOUNTAINS

★ Bratislava

SLOVAKIA

AUSTRIA

Danube River

★ Budapest

HUNGARY

SLOVENIA

CROATIA

SERBIA AND MONTENEGRO

MOLDOVA

CARPATHIAN MOUNTAINS

ROMANIA

UKRAINE

Bucharest ★

Danube River

BLACK SEA

BALKAN MOUNTAINS

★ Sofia

BULGARIA

MACEDONIA

TURKEY

GREECE

People in these countries often decorate Easter eggs with colorful designs.

Poles enjoy an energetic dance called the polka. Often, polka music is played on an accordion.

Cowboys still herd cattle on Hungarian grasslands called pustza. This shepherd watches over his flock.

The Czech Republic has a long tradition of handmade crystal. This man is polishing a crystal vase.

Budapest is the capital of Hungary. It got its name from the former cities of Buda and Obuda on the west side of the Danube River and Pest on the east.

This is the Parliament building on the Danube.

A cable car takes astronomers to Skalnaté-Pleso Observatory in the High Tatra Mountains of Slovakia.

Nadia Comaneci is a famous gymnast from Romania. She won three Olympic gold medals in 1976 when she was only 14.

Rose oil is drawn from fresh rose petals. It has a sweet, earthy fragrance.

Bulgarian rose oil

Country	Area sq mi (sq km)	Population	Language	Government	Currency
Bulgaria	42,822 (110,909)	7,450,349	Bulgarian	Parliamentary Democracy	Lev
Czech Republic	30,387 (78,702)	10,241,138	Czech	Parliamentary Democracy	Koruna
Hungary	35,919 (93,030)	10,006,835	Hungarian	Democratic Constitutional Republic	Forint
Poland	120,727 (312,689)	38,635,144	Polish	Republic	Zloty
Romania	91,699 (237,423)	22,329,977	Romanian	Republic	Lev
Slovakia	18,859 (48,845)	5,431,363	Slovak	Parliamentary Democracy	Koruna

South Central Europe

Bosnia-Herzegovina • Croatia
Serbia and Montenegro • Slovenia

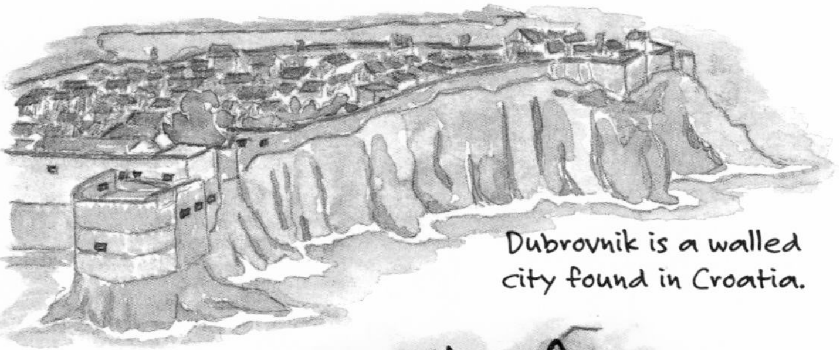

Dubrovnik is a walled city found in Croatia.

A view of the Adriatic Sea from the ancient city of Dubrovnik

Slovenia has a 10-day celebration of spring called Kurenti.

In Serbia and Montenegro, people do a traditional dance called the Cocek.

During Kurenti, people dress up like sheep and chase winter away with clubs and cowbells.

A castle has been on this rocky site in Postojna, Slovenia, since 1201.

This is a statue on Dragon Bridge in Ljubljana, Slovenia.

Beneath the castle is the underworld of Postojna cave.

Postojna cave has been carved and shaped over millions of years by water... drop by drop.

Map labels: ITALY, AUSTRIA, SLOVENIA, Ljubljana, Postojna, Sezana, Zagreb, CROATIA, HUNGARY, DINARIC ALPS, BOSNIA-HERZEGOVINA, Sarajevo, Mostar, ADRIATIC SEA, Dubrovnik, Danube River, Belgrade, ROMANIA, Iron Gates, SERBIA AND MONTENEGRO, BULGARIA, ALBANIA, MACEDONIA

The chamois is a goatlike animal that lives in the high mountains of Slovenia.

For more than 400 years, a special breed of horse called Lipizzaner have been raised near Sezana in Slovenia.

This Lipizzaner is doing a jump called a capriole.

Lipizzaners are usually born dark gray but become a brilliant white when full grown.

Doughnuts dusted with powdered sugar are popular in Slovenia. They are called "Pustni Krofi."

This bridge in Mostar, Bosnia-Herzegovina, was originally built in the 16th century.

In Serbia and Montenegro, the Danube River travels through a narrow passage called the Iron Gates.

Skiing is a popular sport in the Dinaric Alps in Croatia.

Country	Area sq mi (sq km)	Population	Language	Government	Currency
Bosnia-Herzegovina	19,904 (51,750)	4,025,476	Serbo-Croatian	Parliamentary Democratic Republic	Dinar
Croatia	21,829 (56,538)	4,495,904	Croatian	Presidential/Parliamentary Democracy	Kuna
Serbia and Montenegro	39,517 (102,349)	10,829,175	Serbo-Croatian	Republic	New Dinar
Slovenia	7,821 (20,256)	2,011,070	Slovene	Emerging Federal Democratic Republic	Tolar

Southern Europe

Italy • Malta • San Marino • Vatican City

Italy is a boot-shaped country on the Mediterranean Sea. It is a peninsula with water on three sides.

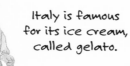

Italy is famous for its ice cream, called gelato.

AUSTRIA

SWITZERLAND

ALPS

FRANCE

Dufour Peak

SLOVENIA

Venice
Trieste

ITALY

Many Italians love all types of car racing.

Corsica (FRANCE)

Pisa

SAN MARINO

San Marino is a tiny country on a mountaintop surrounded by Italy.

Tiber River

ADRIATIC SEA

Rome

VATICAN CITY

MEDITERRANEAN SEA

Sardinia

In Italy, during the 1300s, there was a rediscovery of art and learning called the Renaissance. Great artists, sculptors, architects, writers, and thinkers lived in Italy during this time.

Naples
Mt. Vesuvius
Pompeii

Venice is a city of islands. Gondolas are boats used to travel the city's canals.

The Maltese cross was the banner carried by knights who once lived on the island of Malta. Some firefighters still use this symbol of strength and kindness.

Sicily

Dufour Peak is the highest peak in the Italian Alps. It is 15,203 feet (4,634 m) high.

Valletta

MALTA

Vesuvius is a volcano that erupted in A.D. 79 and buried the city of Pompeii.

Italy makes and exports more than 420 kinds of pasta.

The Leaning Tower of Pisa is a famous marble bell tower that tips to one side.

Italy was the center of the great Roman Empire that spread throughout much of Europe, the Middle East, and North Africa from about A.D. 100 to 476.

In 1883, an Italian writer, Carlo Collodi, met a naughty boy who inspired his story "Pinocchio."

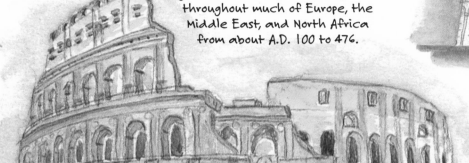

The Colosseum is an old Roman amphitheater. It is where Romans gathered to watch gladiators fight with each other.

Vatican City, in Rome, is the center of the Roman Catholic Church and home to the pope. It is the world's smallest country. The largest Christian church in the world, St. Peter's Basilica, is in Vatican City.

Bocce is a popular lawn bowling game.

Naples is considered the birthplace of pizza.

Country	Area sq mi (sq km)	Population	Language	Government	Currency
Italy	116,324 (301,277)	58,103,033	Italian	Republic	Euro
Malta	122 (316)	398,534	Maltese/English	Republic	Lira
San Marino	24 (62)	28,880	Italian	Independent Republic	Euro
Vatican City	0.17 (0.44)	921	Italian/Latin	Ecclesiastical	Euro

Greece, Albania, and Macedonia

This Greek man is dressed in a traditional costume.

Olive oil is an important Greek export.

Greece is a warm, sunny country with more than 3,000 islands.

Much of Greece has good places to graze sheep and grow olive trees.

He is holding a bouzouki, a Greek folk instrument played like a guitar.

Most Macedonians and Albanians live on small farms.

The ancient Greeks started the Olympic Games to honor their god Zeus.

They raise cattle, hogs, sheep, and poultry.

The winners were crowned with a wreath of laurel leaves as a prize.

When walking in the countryside, you will be greeted warmly by people you meet.

This is a ferryboat. It's the only way people and cars can get to many of the Greek islands.

SERBIA AND MONTENEGRO

Skopje
MACEDONIA

BULGARIA

Tiranë

ALBANIA Lake Ohrid

GREECE

AEGEAN SEA

TURKEY

Athens

Rhodes

Thíra

MEDITERRANEAN SEA

Crete

This is souvlaki, or pork roasted on a long wooden stick.

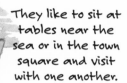

Greeks meet friends at outdoor tavernas.

They like to sit at tables near the sea or in the town square and visit with one another.

The Greeks use colored tiles to create pictures called mosaics.

This is a mosaic of a young girl.

This ancient temple is called the Parthenon. It sits on top of the Acropolis.

These are the ruins of the Acropolis (or high point) in Athens, the capital of Greece.

This is Lake Ohrid, the oldest lake in Europe.

On the island of Crete, old stone windmills are sometimes still used to grind wheat.

The lake is shared by Albania and Macedonia.

At Greek weddings, it is common to do a dance called the Kalamatiano.

The groom is linked to the bride with a handkerchief and leads friends and relatives in a dance.

In 1650 B.C., a volcanic eruption destroyed the once-round island of Santorini. The center of the island sank into the sea leaving a crescent-shaped island known as Thíra. Thíra is a favorite stop for tourists.

Country	Area sq mi (sq km)	Population	Language	Government	Currency
Albania	11,100 (28,749)	3,563,112	Albanian	Emerging Democracy	Lek
Greece	50,942 (131,940)	10,668,354	Greek	Parliamentary Republic	Euro
Macedonia	9,781 (25,333)	2,054,262	Macedonian	Parliamentary Democracy	Denar

Baltic States & Eastern Europe

Belarus • Estonia • Latvia
Lithuania • Moldova • Ukraine

Since 1366, Vytis has been a symbol of Lithuania's independence.

Vytis, the White Knight

Amber jewelry is common in this region.

These musicians are from Belarus. They wear the traditional dress and felt hats.

Bread and salt are traditional gifts of hospitality in this region.

Red foxes are commonly seen near Ukrainian farms.

Basketball is Lithuania's favorite sport.

This is a farm in Moldova that grows wheat.

This is the entrance to Chişinău, the capital of Moldova. It is called the "City Gate."

Map labels:

BALTIC SEA

ESTONIA
★ Tallinn

LATVIA
★ Riga

LITHUANIA
★ Vilnius
Trakai •

RUSSIAN FEDERATION

RUSSIAN FEDERATION

BELARUS
★ Minsk

POLAND

SLOVAKIA
HUNGARY
ROMANIA

MOLDOVA
★ Chişinău

UKRAINE
★ Kiev

BLACK SEA

Trakai is an island castle in Lithuania. It used to be the capital.

These stamps show the costumes from different areas in Latvia.

There is a great Russian influence in all of these countries. This is a Russian Orthodox church in Belarus.

This boy is waving his Lithuanian flag.

In Estonia, the people of a town often get together to sing traditional songs.

For centuries, this region has been invaded and ruled by its neighbors. However, the people have always kept their own languages, their own traditions, and even their own money.

Milk and dairy products are important in this region. Village people often keep a few animals.

This is a special Ukrainian bread baked for Christmas. It is called kolach.

Country	Area sq mi (sq km)	Population	Language	Government	Currency
Belarus	80,154 (207,599)	10,300,483	Belarus/Russian	Parliamentary Democracy	Ruble
Estonia	17,413 (45,100)	1,322,893	Estonian	Parliamentary Republic	Kroon
Latvia	24,946 (64,610)	2,290,237	Latvian/Russian	Parliamentary Democracy	Lats
Lithuania	25,213 (65,301)	3,596,617	Lithuanian	Republic	Litas
Moldova	13,000 (33,700)	4,455,421	Romanian	Republic	Leu
Ukraine	233,100 (603,700)	47,425,336	Ukrainian	Republic	Hryvnia

Russian Federation

The Russian Plain stretches east from the Ural Mountains. Many farms are found here because the rich soil helps things grow.

The Russian Federation (often called Russia) is the largest country in the world.

East of the Ural Mountains, it is part of Asia. West of the mountains, it is part of Europe.

Russia's Volga River is the longest river in Europe. Russians call this river "Mother Volga."

Red carnations are a favorite Russian flower.

Russia's Bolshoi Ballet is one of the most famous ballets in the world.

The Kremlin is the name of a fortress first built in Moscow in 1156.

The Kremlin's red walls and 20 towers form one side of Red Square.

St. Basil's Cathedral in Red Square has eight onion-shaped domes.

Red Square is a long plaza in the heart of Moscow where people have assembled for centuries to watch important events and parades.

Many world-champion chess players are from Russia.

FINLAND
ESTONIA
LATVIA
BELARUS
UKRAINE
St. Petersburg
Russian Plain
ARCTIC OCEAN
Moscow
URAL MOUNTAINS
Volga River
RUSSIAN
KAZAKHSTAN
BLACK SEA
GEORGIA
CASPIAN SEA
AZERBAIJAN
CHINA

Temperatures in Siberia can drop to below -90°F (-68°C).

Large herds of reindeer are raised in the cold Russian tundra of Siberia.

ARCTIC OCEAN

Arctic Circle

Siberia

FEDERATION

Czar Peter the Great (1672–1725) made Russia a great world power. He founded the city of St. Petersburg in 1703.

Mt. Klyuchevskaya Sopka

PACIFIC OCEAN

Mount Klyuchevskaya Sopka is the tallest active volcano in Russia. It gives off smoke continuously and is covered with snow year-round.

The rare Siberian tiger can grow up to 10 feet (3.15 m) long and weigh up to 800 pounds (360 kg).

CHINA

MONGOLIA

In 1961, the Russian cosmonaut Yuri Gagarin was the first man to travel in space.

In Siberia, the ground can be frozen up to 3,000 feet (910 m). Whole prehistoric mammoths have been found preserved in the ice.

These Russian nesting dolls are all handmade and hand painted. They are called matryoshka dolls.

Country	Area sq mi (sq km)	Population	Language	Government	Currency
Russian Federation	6,592,800(17,075,352)	143,420,309	Russian	Federation	Ruble

51

Asia

Asia is the largest continent on Earth. It covers one-third of the land on the planet.

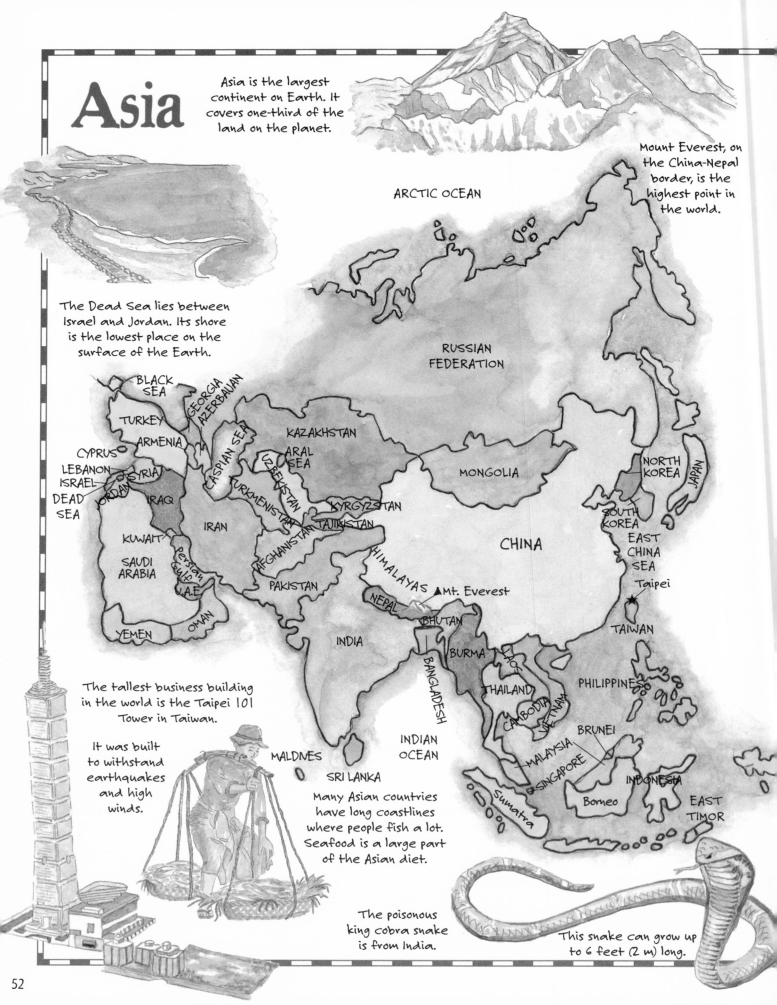

Mount Everest, on the China-Nepal border, is the highest point in the world.

ARCTIC OCEAN

The Dead Sea lies between Israel and Jordan. Its shore is the lowest place on the surface of the Earth.

RUSSIAN FEDERATION

BLACK SEA
GEORGIA
AZERBAIJAN
TURKEY
ARMENIA
CYPRUS
LEBANON
ISRAEL
DEAD SEA
SYRIA
JORDAN
IRAQ
KUWAIT
SAUDI ARABIA
Persian Gulf
U.A.E.
YEMEN
OMAN
IRAN
CASPIAN SEA
UZBEKISTAN
TURKMENISTAN
AFGHANISTAN
PAKISTAN
KAZAKHSTAN
ARAL SEA
KYRGYZSTAN
TAJIKISTAN
MONGOLIA
CHINA
NORTH KOREA
JAPAN
SOUTH KOREA
EAST CHINA SEA
Taipei
TAIWAN
HIMALAYAS
Mt. Everest
NEPAL
BHUTAN
INDIA
BANGLADESH
BURMA
LAOS
THAILAND
CAMBODIA
VIETNAM
PHILIPPINES
BRUNEI
MALAYSIA
SINGAPORE
INDONESIA
Sumatra
Borneo
EAST TIMOR
MALDIVES
SRI LANKA
INDIAN OCEAN

The tallest business building in the world is the Taipei 101 Tower in Taiwan.

It was built to withstand earthquakes and high winds.

Many Asian countries have long coastlines where people fish a lot. Seafood is a large part of the Asian diet.

The poisonous king cobra snake is from India.

This snake can grow up to 6 feet (2 m) long.

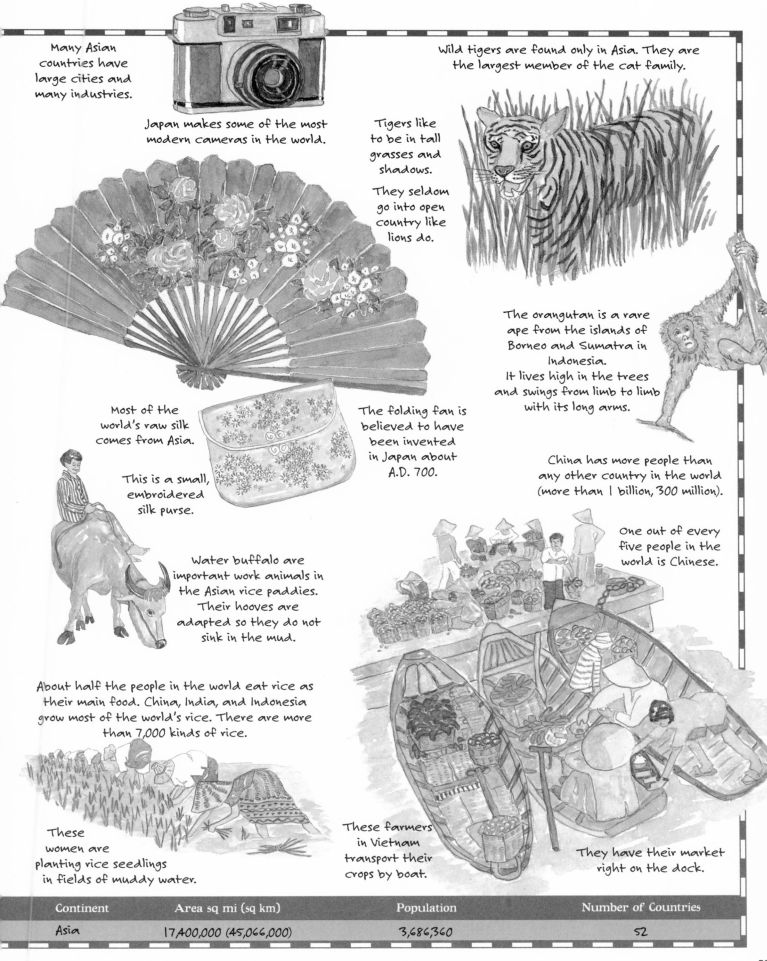

Many Asian countries have large cities and many industries.

Japan makes some of the most modern cameras in the world.

Wild tigers are found only in Asia. They are the largest member of the cat family.

Tigers like to be in tall grasses and shadows.

They seldom go into open country like lions do.

The orangutan is a rare ape from the islands of Borneo and Sumatra in Indonesia.
It lives high in the trees and swings from limb to limb with its long arms.

Most of the world's raw silk comes from Asia.

This is a small, embroidered silk purse.

The folding fan is believed to have been invented in Japan about A.D. 700.

China has more people than any other country in the world (more than 1 billion, 300 million).

One out of every five people in the world is Chinese.

Water buffalo are important work animals in the Asian rice paddies. Their hooves are adapted so they do not sink in the mud.

About half the people in the world eat rice as their main food. China, India, and Indonesia grow most of the world's rice. There are more than 7,000 kinds of rice.

These women are planting rice seedlings in fields of muddy water.

These farmers in Vietnam transport their crops by boat.

They have their market right on the dock.

Continent	Area sq mi (sq km)	Population	Number of Countries
Asia	17,400,000 (45,066,000)	3,686,360	52

Turkey and Cyprus

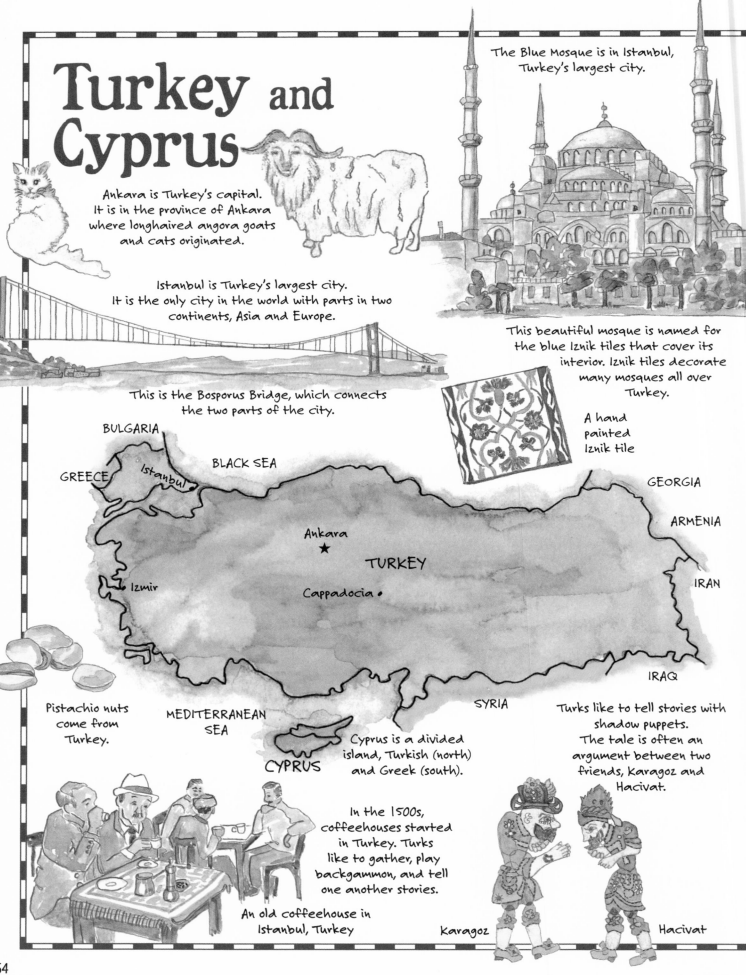

The Blue Mosque is in Istanbul, Turkey's largest city.

Ankara is Turkey's capital. It is in the province of Ankara where longhaired angora goats and cats originated.

Istanbul is Turkey's largest city. It is the only city in the world with parts in two continents, Asia and Europe.

This is the Bosporus Bridge, which connects the two parts of the city.

This beautiful mosque is named for the blue Iznik tiles that cover its interior. Iznik tiles decorate many mosques all over Turkey.

A hand painted Iznik tile

BULGARIA

GREECE

BLACK SEA

Istanbul

GEORGIA

ARMENIA

Ankara

TURKEY

Izmir

Cappadocia

IRAN

IRAQ

Pistachio nuts come from Turkey.

MEDITERRANEAN SEA

SYRIA

CYPRUS

Cyprus is a divided island, Turkish (north) and Greek (south).

Turks like to tell stories with shadow puppets. The tale is often an argument between two friends, Karagoz and Hacivat.

In the 1500s, coffeehouses started in Turkey. Turks like to gather, play backgammon, and tell one another stories.

An old coffeehouse in Istanbul, Turkey

Karagoz

Hacivat

These Turkish women are weaving a carpet.

These are the ruins of an ancient Greek theater near Izmir.

This amphitheater could seat 25,000 people.

Turkey is famous for its beautiful carpets.
A carpet design is unique to the region from which it comes.

Cappadocia is an area in Turkey that was covered by volcanic lava and ash millions of years ago. Homes and underground cities were later carved into the mountains.

Cyprus is on the flying route for more than 220 species of birds. One of them is this Eurasian Griffon Vulture.

A branch of the Islamic religion called the Whirling Dervishes have dancing, music, and fire in their rituals.

Turkey has large plains where crops cannot grow. Small villages of sheepherders are found on the plains.

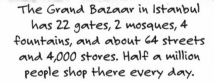

The Grand Bazaar in Istanbul has 22 gates, 2 mosques, 4 fountains, and about 64 streets and 4,000 stores. Half a million people shop there every day.

On a cold morning, this shepherd wears a heavy sheepskin overcoat.

Country	Area sq mi (sq km)	Population	Language	Government	Currency
Cyprus	3,571 (9,249)	780,133	Greek/Turkish	Republic	Pound/Lira
Turkey	301,382 (780,579)	69,660,559	Turkish	Republican Parliamentary Democracy	Lira

Middle East

Israel • Jordan • Lebanon • Syria

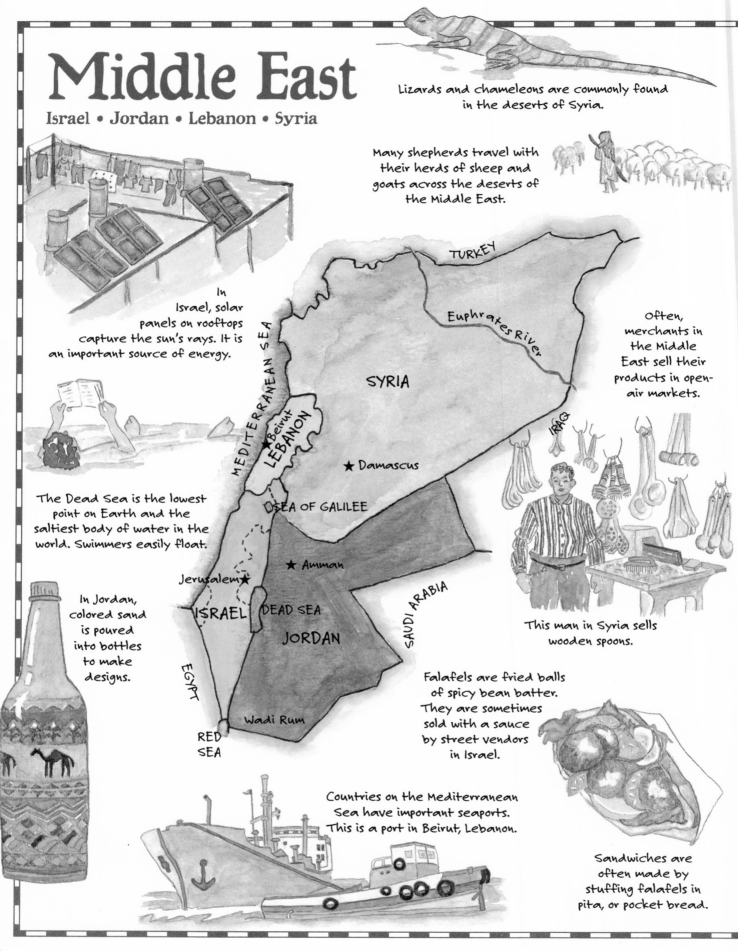

Lizards and chameleons are commonly found in the deserts of Syria.

Many shepherds travel with their herds of sheep and goats across the deserts of the Middle East.

In Israel, solar panels on rooftops capture the sun's rays. It is an important source of energy.

Often, merchants in the Middle East sell their products in open-air markets.

The Dead Sea is the lowest point on Earth and the saltiest body of water in the world. Swimmers easily float.

In Jordan, colored sand is poured into bottles to make designs.

This man in Syria sells wooden spoons.

Falafels are fried balls of spicy bean batter. They are sometimes sold with a sauce by street vendors in Israel.

Countries on the Mediterranean Sea have important seaports. This is a port in Beirut, Lebanon.

Sandwiches are often made by stuffing falafels in pita, or pocket bread.

TURKEY

Euphrates River

SYRIA

MEDITERRANEAN SEA

Beirut LEBANON

★ Damascus

IRAQ

SEA OF GALILEE

★ Amman

Jerusalem ★

ISRAEL

DEAD SEA

JORDAN

SAUDI ARABIA

EGYPT

Wadi Rum

RED SEA

Lake Tiberias is the main source of water for Israel.

It is also called the Sea of Galilee.

Cedar of Lebanon is an evergreen tree found all over Lebanon.

The ruins of Petra

Petra was an ancient city carved in a rock cliff in southern Jordan.

This is a goat hair house—a tent made from animal skins.

It is used by desert Bedouins and can even have cable TV.

Although a lot of cedar of Lebanon trees have been cut down, it is still the national symbol.

The Church of the Holy Sepulcher in Jerusalem is where Christians believe Jesus Christ is buried.

Jerusalem is the capital and largest city in Israel.

Wadi Rum is a desert valley in Jordan.

Lamb is an important meat in the Middle East.

The rock formations there are known as jebels.

The Western Wall is the ruin of a Jewish Temple built in Jerusalem.

This is a street vendor who slices off roasted lamb (called shawarma) to sell.

Country	Area sq mi (sq km)	Population	Language	Government	Currency
Israel	7,876 (20,400)	6,276,883	Hebrew/Arabic	Parliamentary Democracy	New Shekel
Jordan	34,445 (89,213)	5,759,732	Arabic	Constitutional Monarchy	Dinar
Lebanon	4,015 (10,399)	3,826,018	Arabic	Republic	Pound
Syria	71,498 (185,180)	18,448,752	Arabic	Republic	Pound

Near East

Bahrain • Oman • Qatar • Saudi Arabia
United Arab Emirates (UAE) • Yemen

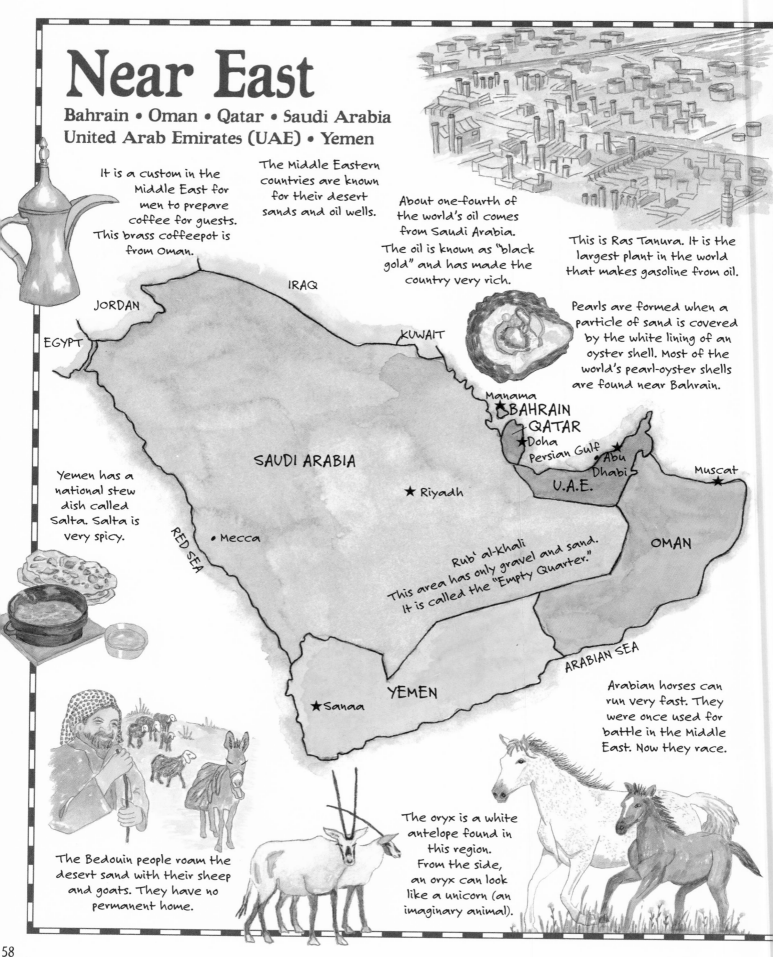

It is a custom in the Middle East for men to prepare coffee for guests. This brass coffeepot is from Oman.

The Middle Eastern countries are known for their desert sands and oil wells.

About one-fourth of the world's oil comes from Saudi Arabia.
The oil is known as "black gold" and has made the country very rich.

This is Ras Tanura. It is the largest plant in the world that makes gasoline from oil.

Pearls are formed when a particle of sand is covered by the white lining of an oyster shell. Most of the world's pearl-oyster shells are found near Bahrain.

IRAQ

JORDAN

EGYPT

KUWAIT

Manama
★ BAHRAIN
QATAR
★ Doha
Persian Gulf
• Abu Dhabi
U.A.E.

Muscat ★

SAUDI ARABIA

★ Riyadh

Yemen has a national stew dish called Salta. Salta is very spicy.

RED SEA

• Mecca

Rub' al-Khali
This area has only gravel and sand. It is called the "Empty Quarter."

OMAN

ARABIAN SEA

YEMEN

★ Sanaa

Arabian horses can run very fast. They were once used for battle in the Middle East. Now they race.

The Bedouin people roam the desert sand with their sheep and goats. They have no permanent home.

The oryx is a white antelope found in this region. From the side, an oryx can look like a unicorn (an imaginary animal).

Camel racing is a popular sport in this desert region. The jockeys are often young boys.

In Oman, a dye called henna is used to decorate women's hands and feet for special occasions like weddings.

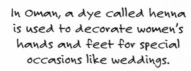

Most people in the Middle East are Muslims who follow the Islamic religion.

Falconers in the Middle East still practice the ancient sport of training birds to hunt for small desert animals.

Men in these countries often wear a red checkered headdress with a black cord.

Dates are thick, sweet fruits that are popular in the Middle East.

Muslims try to make a journey (hajj) once in their lifetime to worship in the Grand Mosque in Mecca, Saudi Arabia.

Camels have long eyelashes that protect their eyes from the sun and sandstorms.

Dates are eaten fresh or dried, with rice, as a dessert, and as a sweetener in drinks.

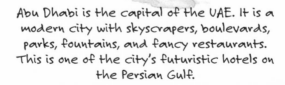

Abu Dhabi is the capital of the UAE. It is a modern city with skyscrapers, boulevards, parks, fountains, and fancy restaurants. This is one of the city's futuristic hotels on the Persian Gulf.

Their two-toed, padded feet do not sink into the sand.

Country	Area sq mi (sq km)	Population	Language	Government	Currency
Bahrain	255 (661)	688,345	Arabic	Constitutional Hereditary Monarchy	Dinar
Oman	82,000 (213,000)	3,001,583	Arabic	Monarchy	Omani Rial
Qatar	4,400 (11,395)	863,051	Arabic	Traditional Monarchy	Qatari Rial
Saudi Arabia	865,000 (2,240,350)	26,417,599	Arabic	Monarchy	Saudi Riyal
U.A.E.	32,000 (82,880)	2,563,212	Arabic	Federation	Emirati Dirham
Yemen	203,849 (527,969)	20,727,063	Arabic	Republic	Rial

Iran, Iraq, and Kuwait

Priests in the Fire Temple in Yazd, Iran, have kept a fire burning in this brass vessel for more than 3,000 years.

This boy and girl live in Baghdad, the capital of Iraq.

Dates are the fruit of the date palm.

Dates are an important crop in Iraq. Dates are sweet and sticky with a hard seed. They are an important part of the diet in many desert countries.

ARMENIA
AZERBAIJAN
CASPIAN SEA
TURKMENISTAN
TURKEY
★Tehran
AFGHANISTAN
SYRIA
Tigris River
Baghdad ★
IRAN
Euphrates River
• Yazd
JORDAN
IRAQ
PAKISTAN
SAUDI ARABIA
KUWAIT
★Kuwait
ARABIAN SEA

These three countries all have vast deserts with large oil deposits.

There are also thousands of camels used for transportation.

In Iran, motorcycles are a common means of transportation.

This is Mount Damavand near Tehran, the capital of Iran.

Ash is the name of a famous, thick Iranian soup that comes in many varieties. Some ash soup can be made with yogurt, noodles, or dried fruit.

Tigris River

The world's first civilization developed on the fertile plain between the Tigris and Euphrates rivers in Iraq.

Euphrates River

The region was called Mesopotamia, which means "between the rivers."

When they have some free time, Iraqi men often enjoy a game of backgammon.

Water is very precious in countries as dry as these. These towers are used to store water in Kuwait.

The wheel and writing were invented in Mesopotamia around 3000 B.C.

Country	Area sq mi (sq km)	Population	Language	Government	Currency
Iran	632,457 (1,638,064)	68,017,860	Persian	Theocratic Republic	Rial
Iraq	167,975 (435,055)	26,074,906	Arabic	Transitional	Dinar
Kuwait	6,880 (17,819)	2,335,648	Arabic	Nominal Constitutional Monarchy	Dinar

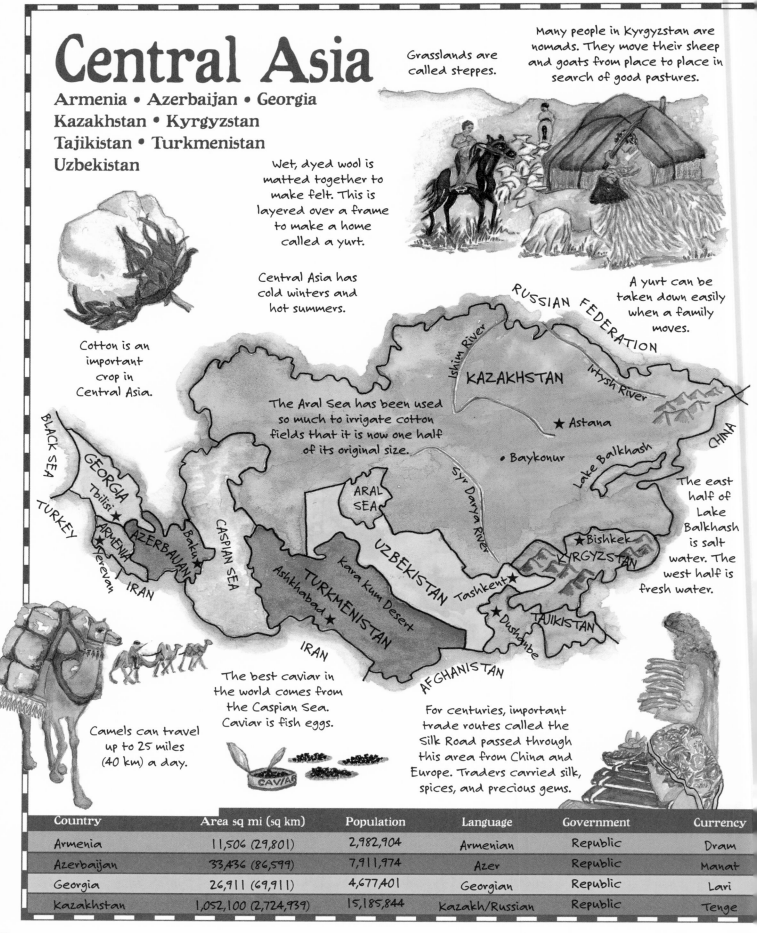

Central Asia

Armenia • Azerbaijan • Georgia
Kazakhstan • Kyrgyzstan
Tajikistan • Turkmenistan
Uzbekistan

Grasslands are called steppes.

Many people in Kyrgyzstan are nomads. They move their sheep and goats from place to place in search of good pastures.

Wet, dyed wool is matted together to make felt. This is layered over a frame to make a home called a yurt.

Central Asia has cold winters and hot summers.

A yurt can be taken down easily when a family moves.

Cotton is an important crop in Central Asia.

The Aral Sea has been used so much to irrigate cotton fields that it is now one half of its original size.

The east half of Lake Balkhash is salt water. The west half is fresh water.

Camels can travel up to 25 miles (40 km) a day.

The best caviar in the world comes from the Caspian Sea. Caviar is fish eggs.

For centuries, important trade routes called the Silk Road passed through this area from China and Europe. Traders carried silk, spices, and precious gems.

RUSSIAN FEDERATION
KAZAKHSTAN
★ Astana
• Baykonur
Lake Balkhash
CHINA
Ishim River
Irtysh River
Syr Darya River
★ Bishkek
KYRGYZSTAN
Tashkent ★
★ Dushanbe
TAJIKISTAN
UZBEKISTAN
ARAL SEA
Kara Kum Desert
Ashkhabad ★
TURKMENISTAN
CASPIAN SEA
BLACK SEA
GEORGIA
Tbilisi ★
ARMENIA
Yerevan ★
AZERBAIJAN
Baku ★
TURKEY
IRAN
IRAN
AFGHANISTAN

Country	Area sq mi (sq km)	Population	Language	Government	Currency
Armenia	11,506 (29,801)	2,982,904	Armenian	Republic	Dram
Azerbaijan	33,436 (86,599)	7,911,974	Azer	Republic	Manat
Georgia	26,911 (69,911)	4,677,401	Georgian	Republic	Lari
Kazakhstan	1,052,100 (2,724,939)	15,185,844	Kazakh/Russian	Republic	Tenge

The people of Central Asia take great pride in their hospitality. They prepare large meals to show respect for their guests.

It is an insult if the guests do not eat enough.

A favorite food is kebabs, made of cubes of meat and vegetables on skewers.

The Armenian alphabet has 38 letters.

Many champion chess players come from this part of the world.

Kazakhstan launched *Sputnik*, the first satellite. It also sent the first man into space and put the MIR space station into orbit.

In Armenia, it is a tradition to tie a piece of cloth to the branch of a tree if you have a problem.

In this part of the world, horses are important possessions. Racehorses, warhorses, and workhorses are well cared for.

Industry is the most important part of Central Asia's economy, causing significant problems with water, air, and land pollution.

Country	Area sq mi (sq km)	Population	Language	Government	Currency
Kyrgyzstan	76,641 (198,500)	5,146,281	Kyrgyz	Republic	Som
Tajikistan	55,251 (143,100)	7,163,506	Tajik	Republic	Somoni
Turkmenistan	188,455 (488,098)	4,952,081	Turkmen	Republic	Manat
Uzbekistan	172,741 (447,399)	26,851,195	Uzbek	Republic	Sum

Afghanistan and Pakistan

Cricket is a popular sport in Pakistan.
It is played by hitting a ball with a flat bat and trying to score runs.

The Kashmir markhor is a wild goat found in Afghanistan and Pakistan. It can climb steep mountain slopes.

TAJIKISTAN

UZBEKISTAN

TURKMENISTAN

CHINA

Mazar-e Sharif

K2

HIMALAYAS

Karakoram Pass

Kabul

AFGHANISTAN

Khyber Pass

Kite flying is popular among Afghan boys.

IRAN

Islamabad

Tea is a favorite drink in both Pakistan and Afghanistan.

Indus River

INDIA

PAKISTAN

An Afghan outdoor market

Tea water is heated in a metal pot called a samovar.

ARABIAN SEA

This is the famous Blue Mosque in the city of Mazar-e Sharif in Afghanistan. The mosque has blue-and-gold-tiled walls.

Naan is a flat bread popular in Afghanistan and Pakistan.

K2 is the name of a mountain near the border of Pakistan, India, and China.

K2 is the second-highest peak in the world.

This group of climbers hopes to make it to the top of K2. The Pakistani men who carry supplies up the mountains for climbers are called porters.

The Khyber Pass is a road through the mountains that connects Pakistan and Afghanistan.

In the 1960s, Pakistan and China worked together to make the Karakoram Pass across the Himalayan Mountains. It follows a section of a route called "The Silk Road."

Pakistani drivers often decorate their trucks and buses with bright colors.

This man is making a sleeping cot by weaving together a thick string and boards. The cot is called a cherpais.

In 1862, the modern game of polo started in this region.

These boys go to a small village school in Pakistan. Boys sit on one side of the classroom and girls sit on the other.

Country	Area sq mi (sq km)	Population	Language	Government	Currency
Afghanistan	251,825 (652,225)	29,928,987	Dari/Pashto	Islamic Republic	Afghani
Pakistan	307,374 (796,095)	162,419,946	Urdu	Federal Republic	Rupee

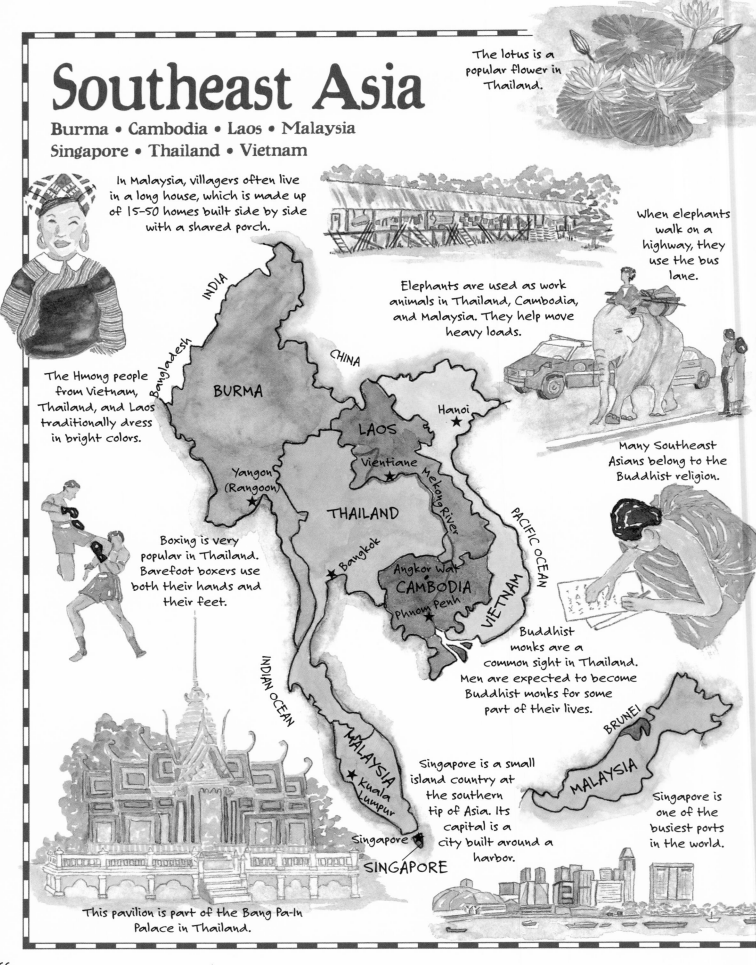

Southeast Asia

Burma • Cambodia • Laos • Malaysia
Singapore • Thailand • Vietnam

The lotus is a popular flower in Thailand.

In Malaysia, villagers often live in a long house, which is made up of 15–50 homes built side by side with a shared porch.

When elephants walk on a highway, they use the bus lane.

Elephants are used as work animals in Thailand, Cambodia, and Malaysia. They help move heavy loads.

The Hmong people from Vietnam, Thailand, and Laos traditionally dress in bright colors.

Many Southeast Asians belong to the Buddhist religion.

Boxing is very popular in Thailand. Barefoot boxers use both their hands and their feet.

Buddhist monks are a common sight in Thailand. Men are expected to become Buddhist monks for some part of their lives.

Singapore is a small island country at the southern tip of Asia. Its capital is a city built around a harbor.

Singapore is one of the busiest ports in the world.

This pavilion is part of the Bang Pa-In Palace in Thailand.

INDIA
Bangladesh
CHINA
BURMA
LAOS
Hanoi
Vientiane
Yangon (Rangoon)
THAILAND
Mekong River
PACIFIC OCEAN
Bangkok
Angkor Wat
CAMBODIA
Phnom Penh
VIETNAM
INDIAN OCEAN
MALAYSIA
Kuala Lumpur
BRUNEI
MALAYSIA
Singapore
SINGAPORE

These Vietnamese farmers take their crops to market in a riverboat called a sampan.

Many families depend on the Mekong River for food and transportation.

Pad thai is one of Thailand's best-known dishes. It is made of stir-fried rice noodles, eggs, fish sauce, and other ingredients.

In Southeast Asian cities, a trishaw is often used for transportation. This is a bicycle attached to a seat for two or more people.

The durian is a fruit that smells awful but tastes delicious.

This girl is eating a durian, sometimes called the "King of Fruits."

Rice paddies are found all over Southeast Asia.

This is rice that is ready to harvest.

These are the ruins of the ancient city of Angkor Wat in Cambodia.

The bamboo dance is popular in Southeast Asia.

Two people sit on the ground and clap bamboo poles together in a rhythm.

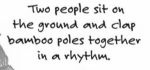

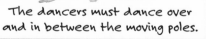

The dancers must dance over and in between the moving poles.

Country	Area sq mi (sq km)	Population	Language	Government	Currency
Burma	261,969 (678,500)	42,909,464	Burmese	Military Junta	Kyat
Cambodia	69,900 (181,041)	13,607,069	Khmer	Multiparty Democracy/ Constitutional Monarchy	Riel
Laos	91,428 (236,799)	6,217,141	Lao	Communist State	Kip
Malaysia	127,316 (329,748)	23,953,136	Malay	Constitutional Monarchy	Ringgit
Singapore	239 (618)	4,492,150	Mandarin/English	Parliamentary Republic	Singapore Dollar
Thailand	198,455 (513,998)	65,444,371	Thai	Constitutional Monarchy	Baht
Vietnam	127,243 (329,559)	83,535,576	Vietnamese	Communist State	Dong

China and Mongolia

China is the third-largest country in the world. It is also home to nearly one billion people. One out of every five people in the world is Chinese.

Table tennis (Ping-Pong) is one of China's most popular sports.

Chinese cities are crowded. Many families live in small apartments with relatives. Pets are often birds.

Mongolia is cold and barren. The people wear woolen tunics and are excellent horse riders.

Emperors ruled China for centuries. In 1974, an emperor's tomb (sealed in 210 B.C.) was found that contained 8,000 life-size clay statues of warriors.

RUSSIAN FEDERATION

KAZAKHSTAN

★ Ulaanbaatar

MONGOLIA

Gobi Desert

KYRGYZSTAN

TAJIKISTAN
AFGHANISTAN
PAKISTAN

HIMALAYAN MOUNTAINS

Plateau of Tibet

The Great Wall

★ Beijing

Huang He River • Tianjin

CHINA

NORTH KOREA

INDIA

Mt. Everest

NEPAL

INDIA
BHUTAN
INDIA

Yangtze River

Shanghai •
Wuhan •

Xi Jiang River

Hong Kong

CHINA SEA

TAIWAN

MYANMAR (BURMA)

LAOS VIETNAM

At 29,035 feet (8,850 m) tall, Mount Everest is the highest mountain in the world.

Many Chinese do t'ai chi exercises in the morning.

Children often exercise as a class when they first get to school.

Chopsticks are used to pinch or scoop up food. The Chinese often eat rice up to three times a day.

The Chinese language has no alphabet. It uses about 5,000 common characters to represent objects and ideas.

Between the 14th and 17th centuries, most of the Great Wall of China was built by hand to keep out invaders.

The wall was originally about 4,000 miles (6,400 km) long, the longest structure ever built.

Many Chinese holidays are celebrated with a dragon parade and fireworks.

Dinosaur eggs were first found in the Gobi Desert of Mongolia.

Many families live and work on sampans, or houseboats, carrying goods up and down the rivers.

Giant pandas live in the bamboo forests of China. Bamboo is a tall grass that can grow more than 18 inches (46 cm) a day. It is the panda's favorite food.

On Chinese farms much of the work is done by hand.

China grows more rice than any other country in the world. Rice seedlings are planted in flooded rice paddies, fields covered with water.

Water buffalo often do the heavy work.

Country	Area sq mi (sq km)	Population	Language	Government	Currency
China	3,696,527 (9,573,998)	1,306,313,812	Mandarin Chinese	Communist State	Renminbi
Mongolia	604,247 (1,565,000)	2,791,272	Khalkha Mongolian	Parliamentary/Presidential	Tugrik

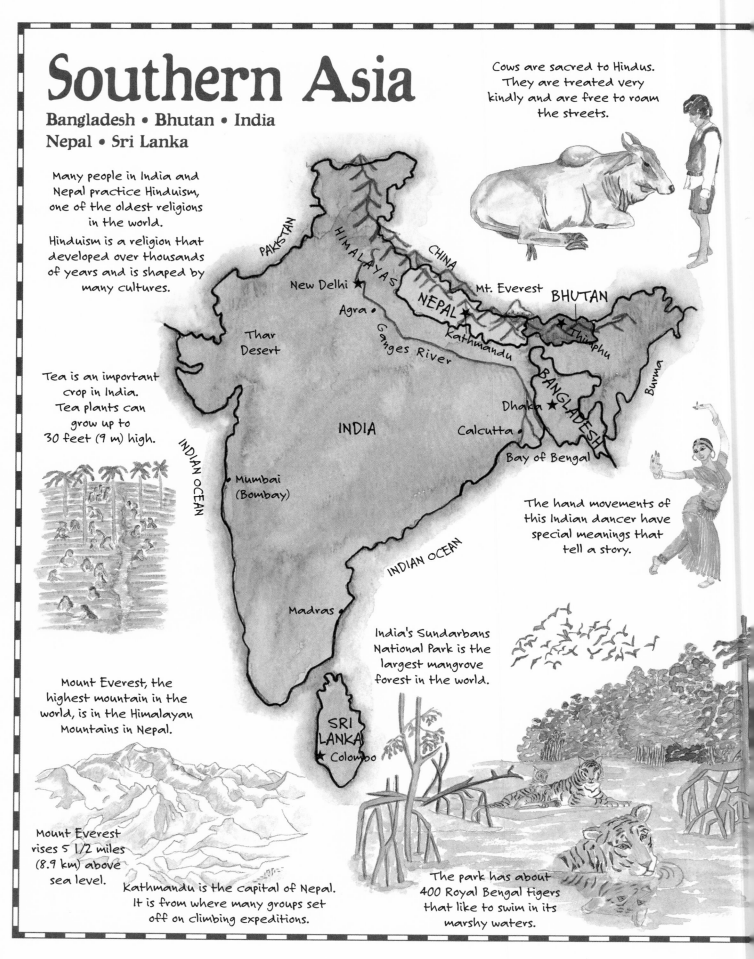

Southern Asia

Bangladesh • Bhutan • India
Nepal • Sri Lanka

Many people in India and Nepal practice Hinduism, one of the oldest religions in the world.

Hinduism is a religion that developed over thousands of years and is shaped by many cultures.

Cows are sacred to Hindus. They are treated very kindly and are free to roam the streets.

Tea is an important crop in India. Tea plants can grow up to 30 feet (9 m) high.

The hand movements of this Indian dancer have special meanings that tell a story.

Mount Everest, the highest mountain in the world, is in the Himalayan Mountains in Nepal.

India's Sundarbans National Park is the largest mangrove forest in the world.

Mount Everest rises 5 1/2 miles (8.9 km) above sea level.

Kathmandu is the capital of Nepal. It is from where many groups set off on climbing expeditions.

The park has about 400 Royal Bengal tigers that like to swim in its marshy waters.

PAKISTAN
HIMALAYAS
CHINA
New Delhi ★
Mt. Everest
NEPAL
BHUTAN
Agra •
Kathmandu ★
Thimphu
Ganges River
Thar Desert
BANGLADESH
Burma
Dhaka ★
Calcutta •
INDIA
Bay of Bengal
INDIAN OCEAN
Mumbai (Bombay) •
INDIAN OCEAN
Madras •
SRI LANKA
★ Colombo

Steam engine trains are common in India. Trains are usually very crowded.

Elephants are often painted and decorated for parades and temple ceremonies.

The Taj Mahal in Agra, India, is considered one of the most beautiful buildings in the world.

It is made of white marble.

Rubber and rubber products are some of Sri Lanka's top exports.

The Asian elephant has an arched back and smaller ears than the African elephant.

This woman drains the milky sap (latex) from the bark of a rubber tree. The latex will be made into rubber.

Holi is a Hindu celebration in the spring where children spray or smear one another with colored powder.

The Taj Mahal is the tomb built for the wife of emperor Shah Jahan between 1632 and 1638.

In Southern Asia, a section of every city is crowded with street vendors. This man weighs flowers to sell in Delhi.

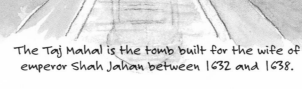

In India, people enjoy going to the movies. Called "Bollywood," India makes more movies than any other country.

Movie billboards are hand painted by groups of artists who specialize in drawing movie stars.

Grown-ups enjoy the fun, too.

Colors for sale

Country	Area sq mi (sq km)	Population	Language	Government	Currency
Bangladesh	55,598 (678,500)	144,319,628	Bengali	Parliamentary Democracy	Taka
Bhutan	18,417 (47,000)	2,232,291	Dzongkha	Monarchy	Ngultrum
India	1,222,243 (3,165,609)	1,080,264,388	Hindi	Federal Republic	Rupee
Nepal	56,827 (147,182)	27,676,547	Nepali	Constitutional Monarchy	Rupee
Sri Lanka	25,332 (65,610)	20,064,776	Sinhala	Republic	Rupee

Eastern Seas

Brunei • East Timor • Indonesia

Traditional houses in East Timor are built on stilts.

Chickens, tools, and firewood are stored under the house.

The wet season in this region is between November and March.

It rains heavily for a very long time.

This is an Indonesian dancer in a traditional ceremonial costume.

Bandar Seri Begawan

BRUNEI

PACIFIC OCEAN

MALAYSIA

SINGAPORE

SUMATRA

MALAYSIA

BORNEO

SULAWESI

IRIAN JAYA

PAPUA NEW GUINEA

Batik is a way to decorate fabric with dye.

It comes from Indonesia.

INDONESIA

Jakarta

JAVA

BALI

Dili

INDIAN OCEAN

EAST TIMOR

Orangutans come from Indonesia.

Many people in Brunei live in the capital city, Bandar Seri Begawan.

Motorcycles are a popular form of transportation in Indonesia.

The number of orangutans has dramatically declined because of forest loss.

This woman is applying a hot wax design to material. When dipped in dye, the wax will not take the color.

Water taxis are boats used to travel up, down, and across the Brunei River in Brunei.

It is believed that early settlers came to the island of Sulawesi by boat and turned their boats into their houses.

The clove tree grows wild in Indonesia.

The spice is actually the dried flower buds.

These cloves are laid out to dry. They have a very strong smell and taste. Cloves are often used to spice meat.

Badminton is a very popular sport in Indonesia.

The Komodo dragon

The Komodo dragon of Indonesia is the largest living lizard in the world.

These women are carrying bundles of harvested rice out of the paddies of Bali, Indonesia.

The Komodo dragon can grow to be more than 10 feet (3 m) long. It is very strong and can run very fast.

These are fishing boats near Bali. They catch lobsters, crabs, and shrimp.

The land is so rich from volcanic ash on some islands that there can be three rice crops a year.

Country	Area sq mi (sq km)	Population	Language	Government	Currency
Brunei	2,228 (5,771)	372,361	Malay	Constitutional Sultanate	Dollar
East Timor	5,743 (14,874)	1,040,880	Tetum	Republic	Dollar
Indonesia	735,309 (1,904,450)	241,973,879	Bahasa Indonesia	Republic	Rupiah

Philippines

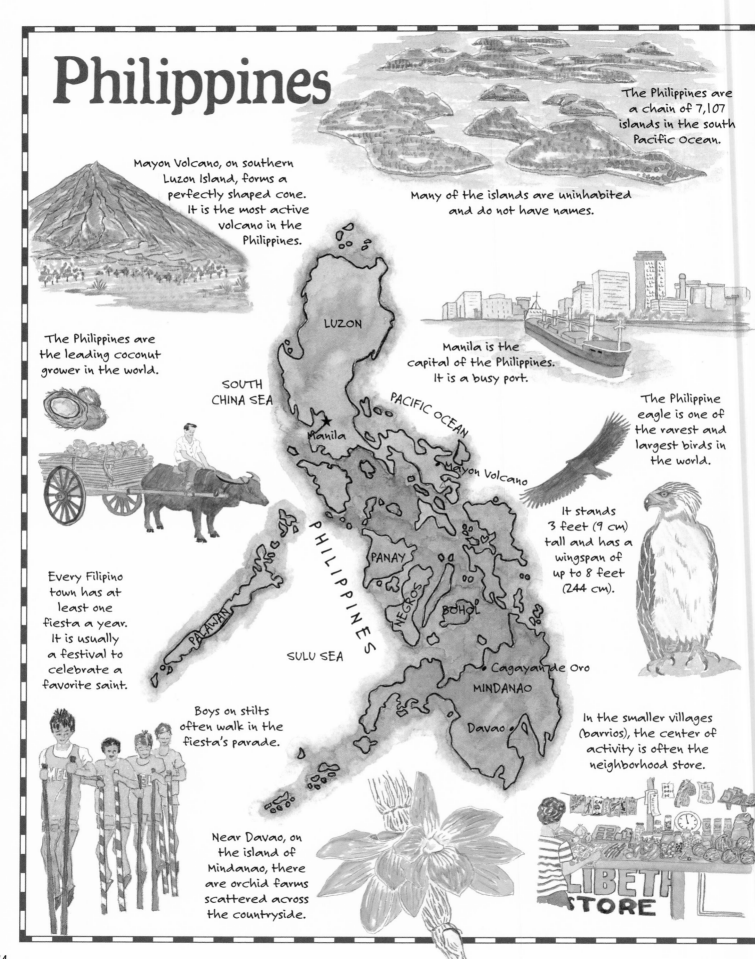

The Philippines are a chain of 7,107 islands in the south Pacific Ocean.

Many of the islands are uninhabited and do not have names.

Mayon Volcano, on southern Luzon Island, forms a perfectly shaped cone. It is the most active volcano in the Philippines.

The Philippines are the leading coconut grower in the world.

Manila is the capital of the Philippines. It is a busy port.

The Philippine eagle is one of the rarest and largest birds in the world.

It stands 3 feet (9 cm) tall and has a wingspan of up to 8 feet (244 cm).

Every Filipino town has at least one fiesta a year. It is usually a festival to celebrate a favorite saint.

Boys on stilts often walk in the fiesta's parade.

In the smaller villages (barrios), the center of activity is often the neighborhood store.

Near Davao, on the island of Mindanao, there are orchid farms scattered across the countryside.

LUZON

SOUTH CHINA SEA

PACIFIC OCEAN

Manila

Mayon Volcano

PANAY

NEGROS

BOHOL

PALAWAN

PHILIPPINES

SULU SEA

Cagayan de Oro

MINDANAO

Davao

LIBETH STORE

MEL

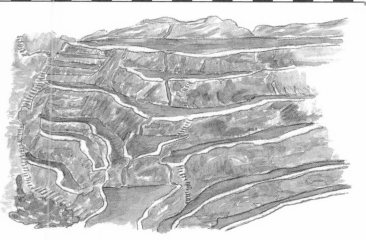

Chocolate Hills

On the island of Bohol there are more than 1,200 small hills. In the summer when it gets very hot and dry, the grass turns brown. The hills look like chocolate candies.

Rice is an important food in the Filipino diet. More than 2,000 years ago, farmers dug out steps in the mountains to make flat places to grow their rice. These are called rice terraces.

Here is a woman using a back-strap loom to weave.

This technique has been used in the Philippines for hundreds of years.

Vintas are boats with colorful sails. These are found near the island of Mindanao.

This nipa hut is a Filipino bamboo home often used on many islands. Cooking and most activities are done outside.

Near Cagayan de Oro there is a 22,239 acre (90 km) pineapple plantation.

Filipinos eat a lot of fish.

An important mode of transportation on many islands is the "Jeepney."

Most fishing is done off the islands of Palawan, Negros, Mindanao, and Panay.

The tarsier monkey lives in the Chocolate Hills.

It is one of the smallest monkeys in the world.

This is a jeep made into a long bus, which has been brightly decorated.

Country	Area sq mi (sq km)	Population	Language	Government	Currency
Philippines	115,830 (300,000)	87,857,473	Filipino/English	Republic	Peso

North and South Korea

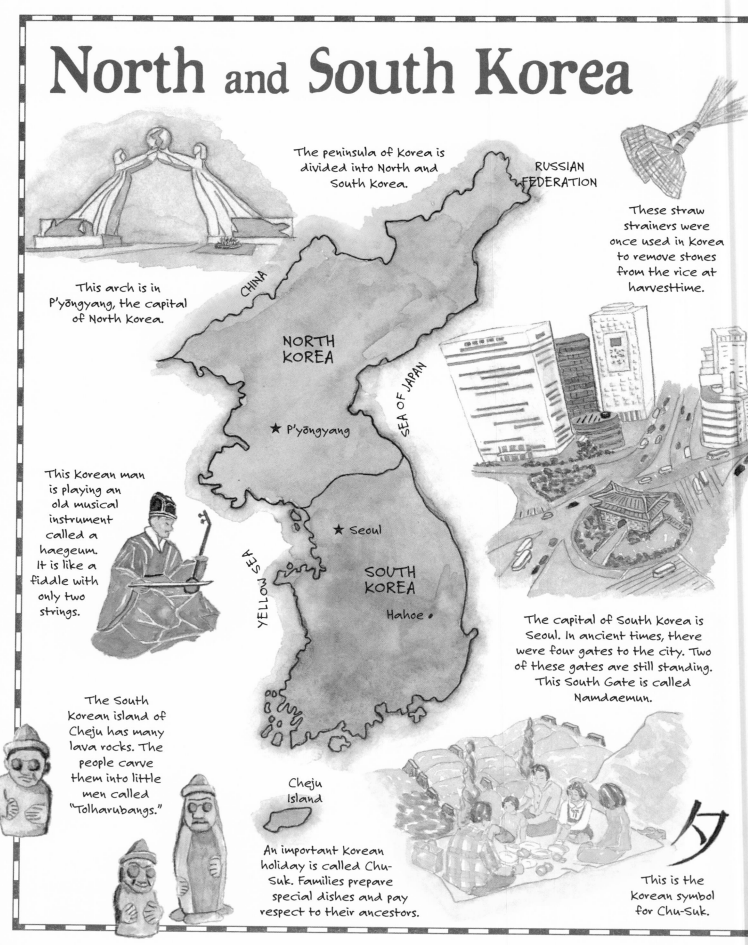

This arch is in P'yŏngyang, the capital of North Korea.

The peninsula of Korea is divided into North and South Korea.

RUSSIAN FEDERATION

These straw strainers were once used in Korea to remove stones from the rice at harvesttime.

CHINA

NORTH KOREA

SEA OF JAPAN

★ P'yŏngyang

This Korean man is playing an old musical instrument called a haegeum. It is like a fiddle with only two strings.

YELLOW SEA

★ Seoul

SOUTH KOREA

Hahoe •

The capital of South Korea is Seoul. In ancient times, there were four gates to the city. Two of these gates are still standing. This South Gate is called Namdaemun.

The South Korean island of Cheju has many lava rocks. The people carve them into little men called "Tolharubangs."

Cheju Island

An important Korean holiday is called Chu-Suk. Families prepare special dishes and pay respect to their ancestors.

This is the Korean symbol for Chu-Suk.

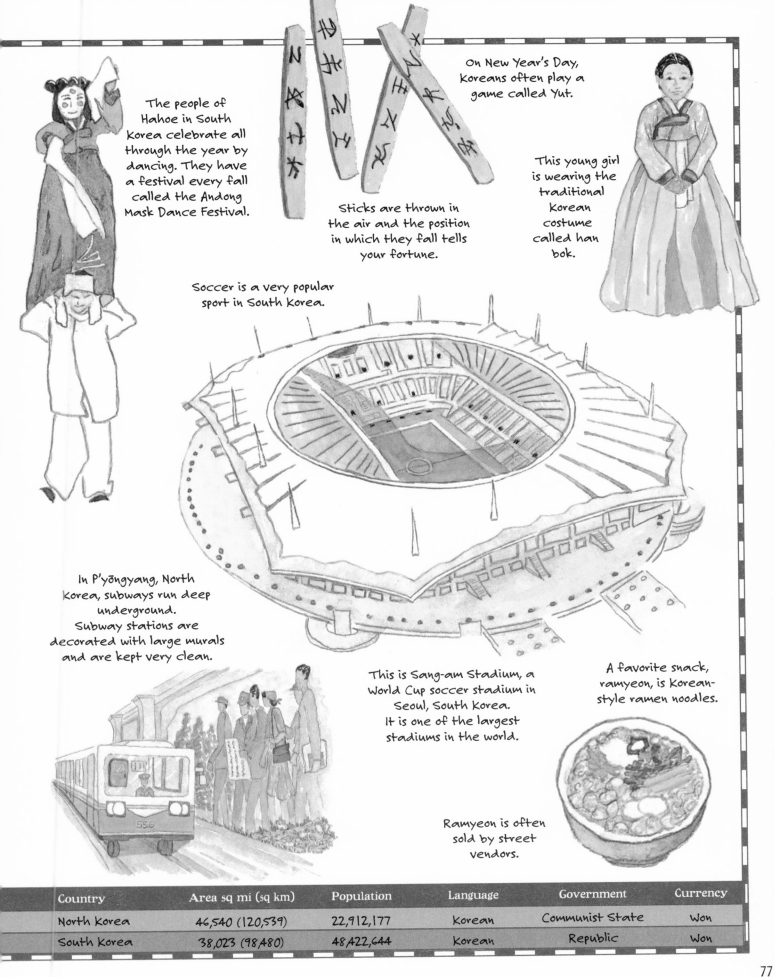

The people of Hahoe in South Korea celebrate all through the year by dancing. They have a festival every fall called the Andong Mask Dance Festival.

Sticks are thrown in the air and the position in which they fall tells your fortune.

On New Year's Day, Koreans often play a game called Yut.

This young girl is wearing the traditional Korean costume called han bok.

Soccer is a very popular sport in South Korea.

In P'yŏngyang, North Korea, subways run deep underground. Subway stations are decorated with large murals and are kept very clean.

This is Sang-am Stadium, a World Cup soccer stadium in Seoul, South Korea. It is one of the largest stadiums in the world.

A favorite snack, ramyeon, is Korean-style ramen noodles.

Ramyeon is often sold by street vendors.

Country	Area sq mi (sq km)	Population	Language	Government	Currency
North Korea	46,540 (120,539)	22,912,177	Korean	Communist State	Won
South Korea	38,023 (98,480)	48,422,644	Korean	Republic	Won

Japan

Mount Fuji, Japan's highest mountain is 12,388 feet (3,776 m) high.

Japan's high-speed trains are known as "bullets." They can travel up to 186 miles per hour (300 kph).

One of Japan's most popular sports is baseball.

Tradition is important in Japan. These women perform a tea ceremony.

Origami is the art of folding paper into shapes.

A kimono is a traditional Japanese garment that both men and women wear on special occasions.

These cranes are made from a folded square of colored paper.

Bowing is a way to greet another person.

Cherry blossoms mark the coming of spring in Japan.

SEA OF JAPAN

JAPAN

Mt. Fuji ▲   Tokyo ★

PACIFIC OCEAN

Japan has more than 77,000 Buddhist temples.

The Japanese like to sit on cushions on the floor. They eat rice at almost every meal.

The Japanese have money called yen. The coins have a hole in them.

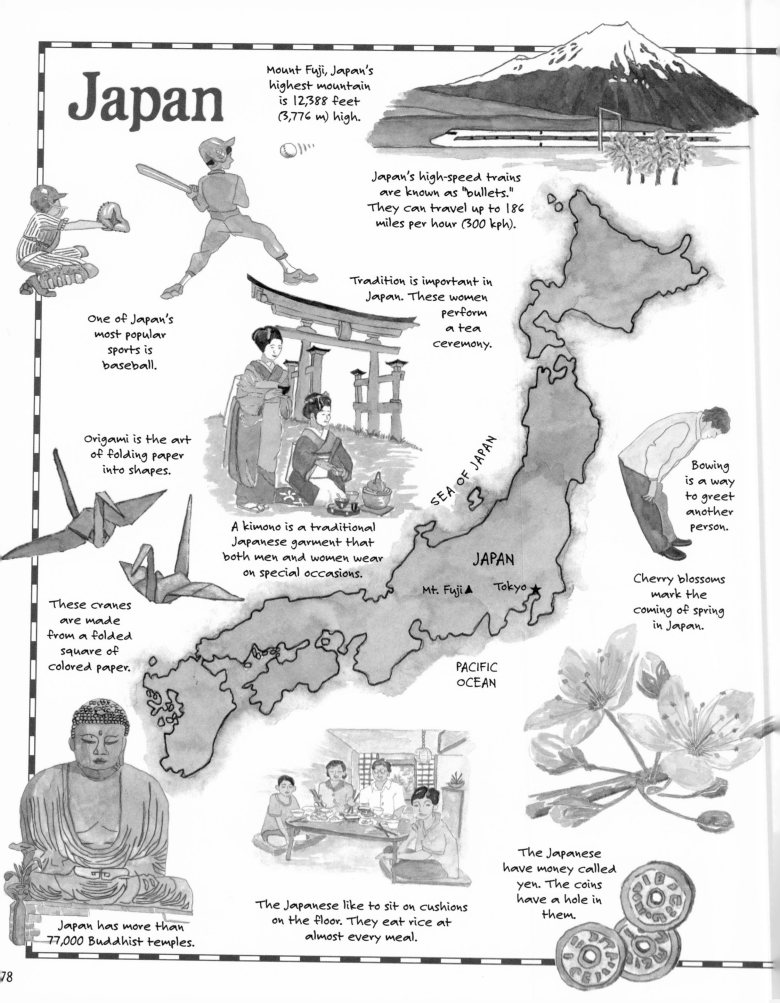

These are fish kites flown on Children's Day, May 5, in Japan.

Sumo wrestlers in Japan are large and powerful. Some weigh almost 400 pounds (181 kg). Japanese people enjoy watching sumo wrestlers.

In Japan, pagodas are religious buildings that have many stories.

人
person

日
sun

木
tree

Flower arranging is popular in Japan. People also grow bonsai, or miniature trees, in their homes.

Deeper bows are for more important people.

Japanese pagodas often have very peaceful gardens.

Japanese writing starts at the top of the page and works down.

Many popular cars are made in Japan. They are shipped to countries all over the world.

There are many small corner stores in Japan. They stay open very late.

Wild snow monkeys live in the mountains of Japan. In winter, they stay warm by sitting in the many natural hot springs.

Country	Area sq mi (sq km)	Population	Language	Government	Currency
Japan	145,882 (377,834)	127,417,244	Japanese	Constitutional Monarchy	Yen

Africa

Africa is made up of 55 countries. It has the world's longest river (the Nile) and largest desert (the Sahara).

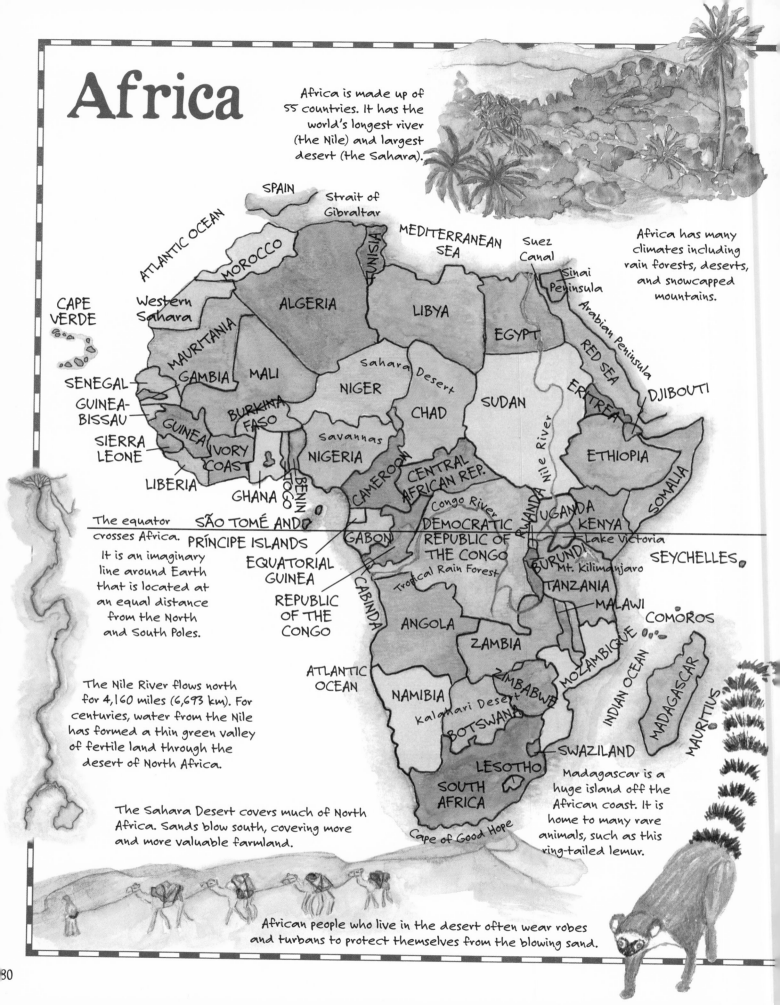

Africa has many climates including rain forests, deserts, and snowcapped mountains.

SPAIN

Strait of Gibraltar

MEDITERRANEAN SEA

Suez Canal

ATLANTIC OCEAN

MOROCCO

TUNISIA

ALGERIA

LIBYA

EGYPT

Sinai Peninsula

Arabian Peninsula

RED SEA

CAPE VERDE

Western Sahara

MAURITANIA

MALI

NIGER

Sahara Desert

CHAD

SUDAN

ERITREA

DJIBOUTI

GAMBIA

SENEGAL

GUINEA-BISSAU

BURKINA FASO

GUINEA

SIERRA LEONE

IVORY COAST

LIBERIA

Savannas

NIGERIA

CENTRAL AFRICAN REP.

ETHIOPIA

SOMALIA

GHANA

TOGO

BENIN

CAMEROON

Nile River

The equator crosses Africa.

SÃO TOMÉ AND PRÍNCIPE ISLANDS

Congo River

DEMOCRATIC REPUBLIC OF THE CONGO

RWANDA

UGANDA

KENYA

Lake Victoria

SEYCHELLES

It is an imaginary line around Earth that is located at an equal distance from the North and South Poles.

GABON

EQUATORIAL GUINEA

REPUBLIC OF THE CONGO

CABINDA

Tropical Rain Forest

BURUNDI

Mt. Kilimanjaro

TANZANIA

MALAWI

COMOROS

ANGOLA

ZAMBIA

MOZAMBIQUE

INDIAN OCEAN

MADAGASCAR

MAURITIUS

The Nile River flows north for 4,160 miles (6,693 km). For centuries, water from the Nile has formed a thin green valley of fertile land through the desert of North Africa.

ATLANTIC OCEAN

NAMIBIA

ZIMBABWE

Kalahari Desert

BOTSWANA

SWAZILAND

LESOTHO

SOUTH AFRICA

Cape of Good Hope

Madagascar is a huge island off the African coast. It is home to many rare animals, such as this ring-tailed lemur.

The Sahara Desert covers much of North Africa. Sands blow south, covering more and more valuable farmland.

African people who live in the desert often wear robes and turbans to protect themselves from the blowing sand.

An African drumbeater

This hourglass drum can be carried under the player's arm.

Egypt's Suez Canal, completed in 1869, gave boats a shortcut between Europe and Asia.

In order to protect some of the world's most spectacular animals, Africa has many game parks where animals cannot be hunted.

African Pygmies are hunters and gatherers. They live in the rain forests and rely on the forest for their food, clothing, and shelter.

The African elephant is the largest land animal in the world. It has a dip in its back and large ears that cover its shoulders.

About 2/3 of Africans live in rural areas.

Soccer (also called football) is a favorite team sport all over Africa.

Fruits, vegetables, and grains are sold in open markets throughout Africa.

Continent	Area sq mi (sq km)	Population	Number of Countries
Africa	11,724,300 (30,365,700)	906,000,000	55

North Africa

Algeria • Egypt • Libya • Morocco
Sudan • Tunisia

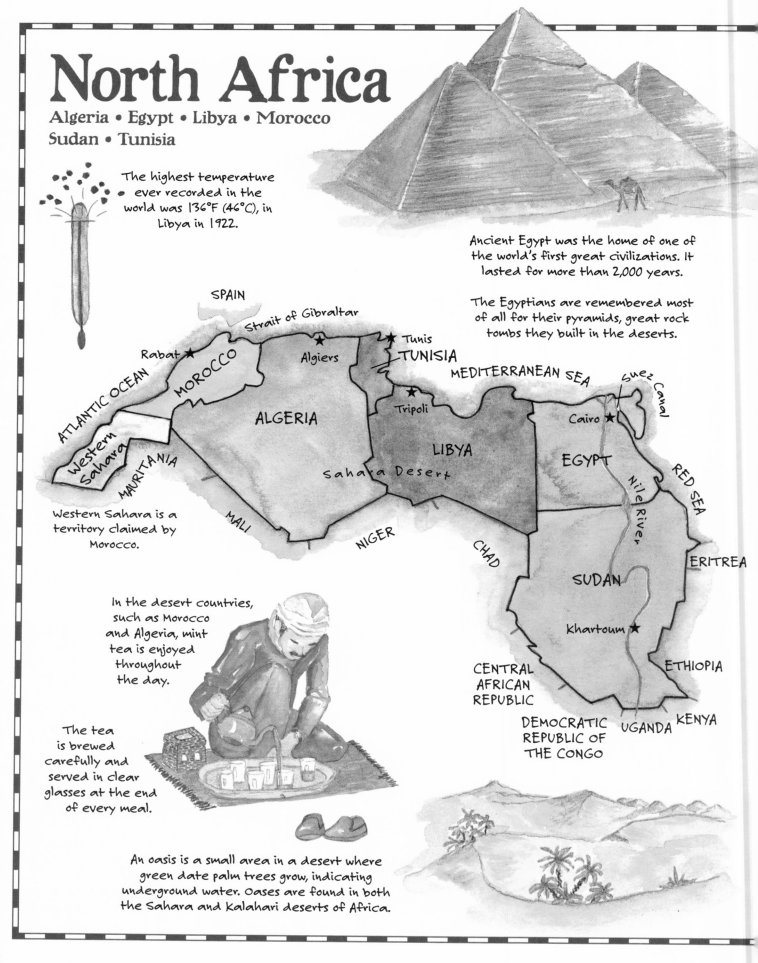

The highest temperature ever recorded in the world was 136°F (46°C), in Libya in 1922.

Ancient Egypt was the home of one of the world's first great civilizations. It lasted for more than 2,000 years.

The Egyptians are remembered most of all for their pyramids, great rock tombs they built in the deserts.

SPAIN

Strait of Gibraltar

Rabat ★

MOROCCO

Algiers ★

Tunis ★
TUNISIA

MEDITERRANEAN SEA

Suez Canal

ATLANTIC OCEAN

Western Sahara

MAURITANIA

ALGERIA

Tripoli ★

LIBYA

Sahara Desert

Cairo ★

EGYPT

RED SEA

Nile River

MALI

NIGER

CHAD

ERITREA

SUDAN

Western Sahara is a territory claimed by Morocco.

In the desert countries, such as Morocco and Algeria, mint tea is enjoyed throughout the day.

Khartoum ★

CENTRAL AFRICAN REPUBLIC

ETHIOPIA

The tea is brewed carefully and served in clear glasses at the end of every meal.

DEMOCRATIC REPUBLIC OF THE CONGO

UGANDA

KENYA

An oasis is a small area in a desert where green date palm trees grow, indicating underground water. Oases are found in both the Sahara and Kalahari deserts of Africa.

The gold mask of King Tut

This minaret is on the Mosque at Khartoum in Sudan.

The Arab dhows, sturdy sailing crafts, have been on the Nile River for centuries.

Mosques are places of worship for Muslims. They have very tall towers (minarets).

The Hand of Fatima is a symbol often used in jewelry to protect the wearer.

Tutankhamen was nine years old when he became king of Egypt. He is known as King Tut. He died when he was 18 and was buried and forgotten for 3,000 years.

In 1922, King Tut's tomb was rediscovered. It contained about 5,000 treasures, including the mummy of the "boy-king" and a lifelike gold mask.

Wherever they are, Muslims kneel and pray five times a day, facing east toward Mecca, Saudi Arabia, the birthplace of the prophet Mohammed.

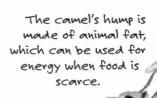

The camel's hump is made of animal fat, which can be used for energy when food is scarce.

An African camel is called a dromedary and has only one hump.

In a small village in the Sahara Desert, these children learn Arabic under a shady tree in an outdoor classroom.

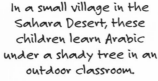

Camels are still used for travel in the desert and also for racing.

Country	Area sq mi (sq km)	Population	Language	Government	Currency
Algeria	919,595 (2,381,751)	32,531,853	Arabic	Republic	Dinar
Egypt	385,299 (997,743)	77,505,756	Arabic	Republic	Pound
Libya	679,358 (1,759,537)	5,765,563	Arabic	Jamahiriya	Dinar
Morocco	177,117 (458,733)	32,725,847	Arabic	Constitutional Monarchy	Dirham
Sudan	967,493 (2,505,807)	40,187,486	Arabic	Authoritarian Regime	Pound
Tunisia	63,170 (163,610)	10,074,951	Arabic	Republic	Dinar

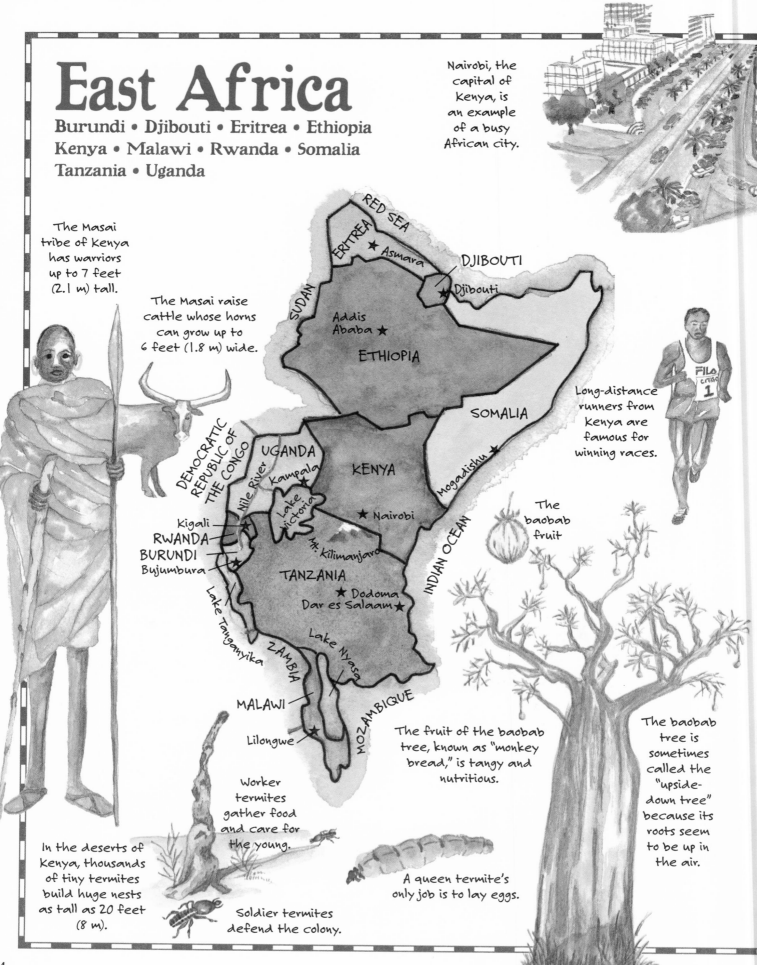

East Africa

Burundi • Djibouti • Eritrea • Ethiopia
Kenya • Malawi • Rwanda • Somalia
Tanzania • Uganda

Nairobi, the capital of Kenya, is an example of a busy African city.

The Masai tribe of Kenya has warriors up to 7 feet (2.1 m) tall.

The Masai raise cattle whose horns can grow up to 6 feet (1.8 m) wide.

RED SEA

ERITREA

★ Asmara

DJIBOUTI

★ Djibouti

SUDAN

Addis Ababa ★

ETHIOPIA

SOMALIA

DEMOCRATIC REPUBLIC OF THE CONGO

UGANDA

★ Kampala

Nile River

Lake Victoria

KENYA

★ Mogadishu

Long-distance runners from Kenya are famous for winning races.

The baobab fruit

Kigali
RWANDA
BURUNDI
Bujumbura

★ Nairobi

Mt. Kilimanjaro

INDIAN OCEAN

Lake Tanganyika

TANZANIA

★ Dodoma
Dar es Salaam ★

Lake Nyasa

ZAMBIA

MALAWI

MOZAMBIQUE

★ Lilongwe

The fruit of the baobab tree, known as "monkey bread," is tangy and nutritious.

The baobab tree is sometimes called the "upside-down tree" because its roots seem to be up in the air.

In the deserts of Kenya, thousands of tiny termites build huge nests as tall as 20 feet (8 m).

Worker termites gather food and care for the young.

Soldier termites defend the colony.

A queen termite's only job is to lay eggs.

Mount Kilimanjaro is Africa's highest point. It is a snowcapped mountain rising 19,340 feet (5,895 m), near the equator in Tanzania.

The lush grasses of the savannas are where many wild animals live and graze.

An acacia tree

There are two kinds of rhinoceroses in Africa, black and white.

Kenya's animal wildlife is an important tourist attraction.

Giraffes are the tallest animals in the world. Males can grow up to 18 feet (5 m) tall.

A white rhinoceros can grow up to 6 feet (1.8 m) tall and 15 feet (4.6 m) long.

Safaris are guided tours that take visitors to see animals living in the wild. The tourists take pictures of the animals.

Male lions have the furry mane, but female lions are the hunters.

Young lions are called cubs.

These East African dancers leap straight up in the air and shake their shoulders before they come down again.

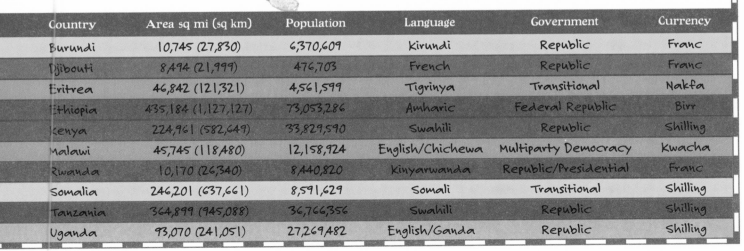

Country	Area sq mi (sq km)	Population	Language	Government	Currency
Burundi	10,745 (27,830)	6,370,609	Kirundi	Republic	Franc
Djibouti	8,494 (21,999)	476,703	French	Republic	Franc
Eritrea	46,842 (121,321)	4,561,599	Tigrinya	Transitional	Nakfa
Ethiopia	435,184 (1,127,127)	73,053,286	Amharic	Federal Republic	Birr
Kenya	224,961 (582,649)	33,829,590	Swahili	Republic	Shilling
Malawi	45,745 (118,480)	12,158,924	English/Chichewa	Multiparty Democracy	Kwacha
Rwanda	10,170 (26,340)	8,440,820	Kinyarwanda	Republic/Presidential	Franc
Somalia	246,201 (637,661)	8,591,629	Somali	Transitional	Shilling
Tanzania	364,899 (945,088)	36,766,356	Swahili	Republic	Shilling
Uganda	93,070 (241,051)	27,269,482	English/Ganda	Republic	Shilling

West Africa

Benin • Burkina Faso • Cameroon
Cape Verde • Chad • Gambia • Ghana
Guinea • Guinea-Bissau • Ivory Coast
Liberia • Mali • Mauritania • Niger
Nigeria • Senegal • Sierra Leone • Togo

The cacao tree grows in the African tropics of Ghana, Nigeria, and the Ivory Coast.

Chocolate is made from the small cacao beans found inside the pods, which hang from the limbs of the cacao tree.

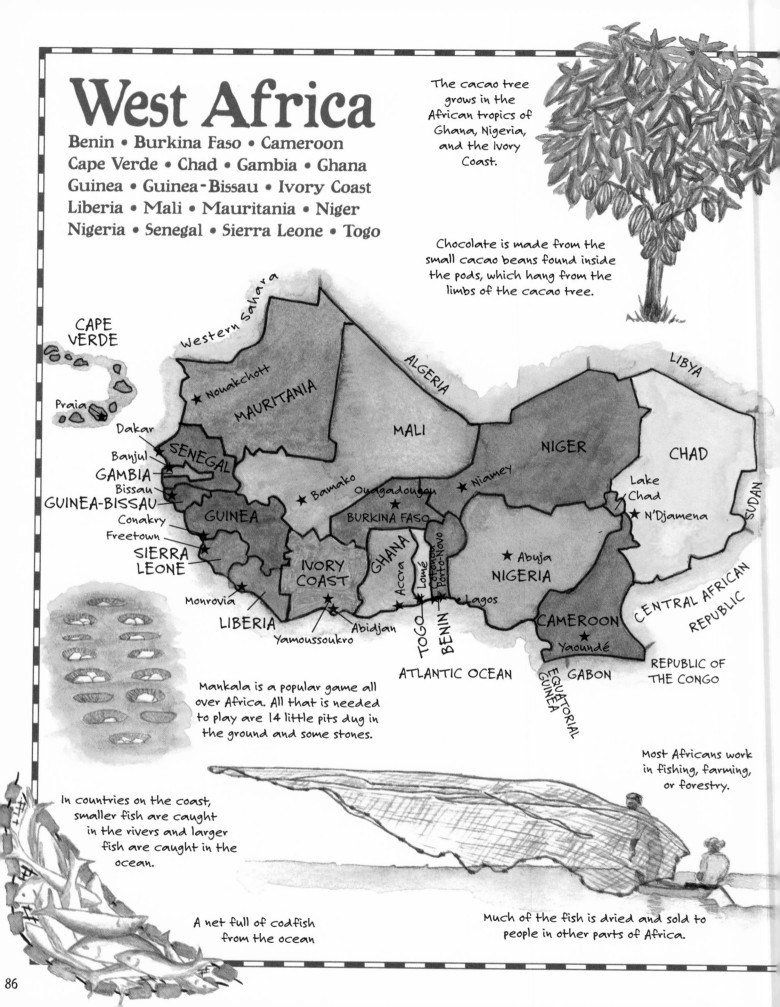

CAPE VERDE

Praia

Western Sahara

ALGERIA

LIBYA

Nouakchott

MAURITANIA

MALI

NIGER

CHAD

SUDAN

Dakar

SENEGAL

Banjul

GAMBIA

Bissau

GUINEA-BISSAU

Conakry

GUINEA

Freetown

SIERRA LEONE

Bamako

Ouagadougou

BURKINA FASO

Niamey

Lake Chad

N'Djamena

Monrovia

LIBERIA

IVORY COAST

Yamoussoukro

Abidjan

GHANA

Accra

Lomé

Cotonou

Porto-Novo

TOGO

BENIN

Lagos

Abuja

NIGERIA

CENTRAL AFRICAN REPUBLIC

CAMEROON

Yaoundé

EQUATORIAL GUINEA

GABON

REPUBLIC OF THE CONGO

ATLANTIC OCEAN

Mankala is a popular game all over Africa. All that is needed to play are 14 little pits dug in the ground and some stones.

Most Africans work in fishing, farming, or forestry.

In countries on the coast, smaller fish are caught in the rivers and larger fish are caught in the ocean.

A net full of codfish from the ocean

Much of the fish is dried and sold to people in other parts of Africa.

Cornmeal is often ground up with a wooden mortar and pestle.

Ugali is a popular meal. It is a porridge made with cornmeal, salt, and water. It is often served with meat or vegetables.

This is a wooden mask from Burkina Faso.

The high forehead is a sign of intelligence, and the peaks on the head are to capture the wisdom of the world.

This mother is carrying a pail of water in her hand, and a load of coconuts and firewood on her head.

The coconut shells can be used for fuel.

She also tends the family goats.

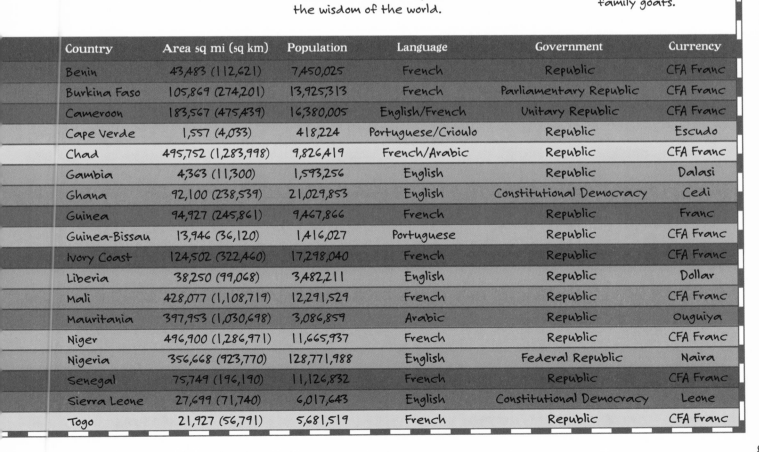

Country	Area sq mi (sq km)	Population	Language	Government	Currency
Benin	43,483 (112,621)	7,450,025	French	Republic	CFA Franc
Burkina Faso	105,869 (274,201)	13,925,313	French	Parliamentary Republic	CFA Franc
Cameroon	183,567 (475,439)	16,380,005	English/French	Unitary Republic	CFA Franc
Cape Verde	1,557 (4,033)	418,224	Portuguese/Crioulo	Republic	Escudo
Chad	495,752 (1,283,998)	9,826,419	French/Arabic	Republic	CFA Franc
Gambia	4,363 (11,300)	1,593,256	English	Republic	Dalasi
Ghana	92,100 (238,539)	21,029,853	English	Constitutional Democracy	Cedi
Guinea	94,927 (245,861)	9,467,866	French	Republic	Franc
Guinea-Bissau	13,946 (36,120)	1,416,027	Portuguese	Republic	CFA Franc
Ivory Coast	124,502 (322,460)	17,298,040	French	Republic	CFA Franc
Liberia	38,250 (99,068)	3,482,211	English	Republic	Dollar
Mali	428,077 (1,108,719)	12,291,529	French	Republic	CFA Franc
Mauritania	397,953 (1,030,698)	3,086,859	Arabic	Republic	Ouguiya
Niger	496,900 (1,286,971)	11,665,937	French	Republic	CFA Franc
Nigeria	356,668 (923,770)	128,771,988	English	Federal Republic	Naira
Senegal	75,749 (196,190)	11,126,832	French	Republic	CFA Franc
Sierra Leone	27,699 (71,740)	6,017,643	English	Constitutional Democracy	Leone
Togo	21,927 (56,791)	5,681,519	French	Republic	CFA Franc

South and Central Africa

Angola • Botswana • Central African
Republic • Democratic Republic of the Congo
Equatorial Guinea • Gabon • Lesotho
Madagascar • Mozambique • Namibia
Republic of the Congo • São Tomé &
Príncipe • South Africa • Swaziland
Zambia • Zimbabwe

The women in the Ndebele tribe of South Africa paint the inside and outside of their homes with simple, bright patterns.

CHAD

SUDAN

CENTRAL AFRICAN REPUBLIC

Bangui ★

CAMEROON

Malabo

EQUATORIAL GUINEA

Libreville ★

GABON

Congo River

REPUBLIC OF THE CONGO

Brazzaville

DEMOCRATIC REPUBLIC OF THE CONGO

Tropical Rain Forest

UGANDA

RWANDA

BURUNDI

TANZANIA

SÃO TOMÉ & PRÍNCIPE

The islands of São Tomé & Príncipe form the smallest country in Africa.

Cabinda (ANGOLA)

Kinshasa

★ Luanda

ATLANTIC OCEAN

ANGOLA

ZAMBIA

Lusaka ★

MALAWI

MOZAMBIQUE

MADAGASCAR

Antananarivo ★

INDIAN OCEAN

Some Africans wear colorful beads.

Beads sometimes have special messages.

NAMIBIA

Windhoek ★

Kalahari Desert

BOTSWANA

Gaborone ★

Harare ●

ZIMBABWE

Pretoria ★

SWAZILAND

Maputo

Mbabane

Bloemfontein ●

SOUTH AFRICA

Maseru

LESOTHO

Cape Town ★

Cape of Good Hope

Many of Africa's forests are being cut down to clear the land for farming, to build houses, and to provide wood for fuel.

A man might give a woman a white necklace to say "I love you."

Victoria Falls is in a 40-mile-long (64 km) canyon on the Zimbabwe/Zambia border. The water falls 355 feet (108 km).

Gorillas, the largest kind of ape, live in the African rain forests. Males can weigh up to 600 pounds (273 kg).

Gorillas usually walk on all fours.

Copper pots

Diamonds are prized for their beauty and their hardness.

Many of the world's diamonds come from African countries like South Africa, Namibia, and Botswana.

In many parts of southern and central Africa, villages are made up of circular thatched huts.

In some small villages, children go to school outside under a shady tree instead of in a classroom.

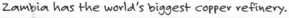

Zambia has the world's biggest copper refinery.

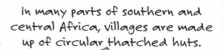

Country	Area sq mi (sq km)	Population	Language	Government	Currency
Angola	481,351 (1,246,699)	11,190,786	Portuguese	Republic	Kwanza
Botswana	224,607 (581,732)	1,640,115	English/Setswana	Parliamentary Republic	Pula
Central African Rep.	240,533 (622,980)	3,799,897	French/Sango	Republic	CFA Franc
Dem. Rep. of the Congo	905,563 (2,345,408)	60,085,804	French/Lingala	Dictatorship	Congolese Franc
Equatorial Guinea	10,830 (28,050)	535,881	French/Spanish	Republic	CFA Franc
Gabon	103,347 (267,669)	1,389,201	French	Republic	CFA Franc
Lesotho	11,718 (30,350)	1,867,035	Sesotho/English	Parliamentary Constitutional Monarchy	Loti
Madagascar	226,656 (587,039)	18,040,341	Malagasy/French	Republic	Franc
Mozambique	309,494 (801,589)	19,406,703	Portuguese/Emakhuwa	Republic	Metical
Namibia	318,694 (825,417)	2,030,692	English/Afrikaans	Republic	Rand
Republic of the Congo	132,046 (341,999)	3,039,126	French/Lingala/Monokutuba	Republic	CFA Franc
São Tomé & Príncipe	372 (964)	187,410	Portuguese	Republic	Dobra
South Africa	471,008 (1,219,911)	44,344,136	Zulu/Xhosa/Afrikaans	Republic	Rand
Swaziland	6,703 (17,361)	1,173,900	English/SiSwate	Monarchy	Lilangeni
Zambia	290,583 (752,607)	11,261,795	English/Bemba	Republic	Kwacha
Zimbabwe	150,803 (390,580)	12,746,990	English/Shona	Parliamentary Democracy	Dollar

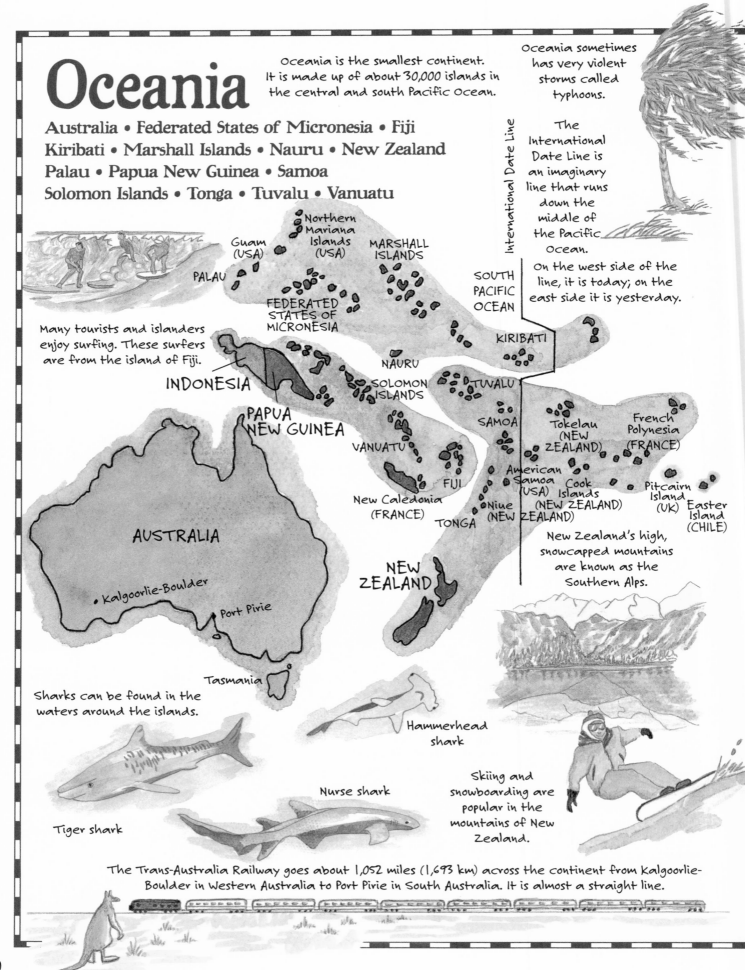

Oceania

Oceania is the smallest continent. It is made up of about 30,000 islands in the central and south Pacific Ocean.

Oceania sometimes has very violent storms called typhoons.

Australia • Federated States of Micronesia • Fiji
Kiribati • Marshall Islands • Nauru • New Zealand
Palau • Papua New Guinea • Samoa
Solomon Islands • Tonga • Tuvalu • Vanuatu

International Date Line

The International Date Line is an imaginary line that runs down the middle of the Pacific Ocean.

On the west side of the line, it is today; on the east side it is yesterday.

Northern Mariana Islands (USA)

Guam (USA)

MARSHALL ISLANDS

PALAU

SOUTH PACIFIC OCEAN

FEDERATED STATES OF MICRONESIA

KIRIBATI

Many tourists and islanders enjoy surfing. These surfers are from the island of Fiji.

NAURU

INDONESIA

SOLOMON ISLANDS

TUVALU

PAPUA NEW GUINEA

SAMOA

Tokelau (NEW ZEALAND)

French Polynesia (FRANCE)

VANUATU

American Samoa (USA)

Cook Islands (NEW ZEALAND)

Pitcairn Island (UK)

Easter Island (CHILE)

FIJI

Niue (NEW ZEALAND)

New Caledonia (FRANCE)

TONGA

New Zealand's high, snowcapped mountains are known as the Southern Alps.

AUSTRALIA

• Kalgoorlie-Boulder

Port Pirie

NEW ZEALAND

Tasmania

Sharks can be found in the waters around the islands.

Hammerhead shark

Tiger shark

Nurse shark

Skiing and snowboarding are popular in the mountains of New Zealand.

The Trans-Australia Railway goes about 1,052 miles (1,693 km) across the continent from Kalgoorlie-Boulder in Western Australia to Port Pirie in South Australia. It is almost a straight line.

These white sand beaches are on the island of Bora Bora in French Polynesia. *Polynesia* means "many islands."

On Easter Sunday in 1722, a Dutch explorer discovered a Pacific island that he called Easter Island.

These are some of the 900 large statues, called moai, that are found on Easter Island. No one knows how they got there.

The Centrepoint Tower in Sydney, Australia, is the second highest structure in the Southern Hemisphere.

If alarmed, this frilled lizard of northern Australia can raise its collar to scare off enemies.

This man from Samoa uses the conch as a trumpet to call islanders together.

This humpback whale is breaching, or leaping out of the water. The humpback whale migrates from Antarctica to spend the winter in the warm waters around Tonga.

The conch is a large tropical sea snail with a spiral shell.

Micronesia means "tiny islands."

Continent	Area sq mi (sq km)	Population	Number of countries
Oceania	3,300,000 (8,547,000)	32,000,000	14

Australia

Australia is known as the "Land Down Under" because it is entirely below the equator. It has many animals found nowhere else in the world.

About 400 kinds of coral and more than 2,000 types of fishes live in the reef's warm waters.

Australia is the smallest of the seven continents.

The Great Barrier Reef is the longest coral reef in the world.

Wombats live only in Australia. They are marsupials, animals whose babies are born, fed, and carried in a pouch on their mother's belly.

Sheep and cattle ranches in the outback can go on for miles. They are called stations.

Ayers Rock suddenly rises all alone out of the middle of the outback desert. It is more than 1,000 feet (335 m) high.

There is an almost 3,500-mile (5,631.5 km) "dog fence" that keeps the dogs out of the southern sheep country.

Australian wild dogs are called dingoes. They often attack sheep.

Windsurfing

Because the weather is warm most of the time, Australians enjoy outdoor sports, especially water sports, cricket, golf, and rugby.

The platypus lives in Australia's rivers. It is a mammal, which means it has fur and feeds milk to its young. It is the only mammal that lays eggs.

The Tasmanian devil is a fierce marsupial. It is found only on the small Australian island of Tasmania.

The Sydney Opera House was built to look like ships sailing into the harbor.

INDIAN OCEAN
PACIFIC OCEAN

Darwin

Alice Springs

AUSTRALIA

Dog fence

Brisbane

Darling River

Sydney

Canberra

Adelaide

Melbourne

Perth

GREAT DIVIDING RANGE

Tasmania

Koalas live in Australia's eucalyptus trees. They eat the leaves of the tree, which give them almost all the water they need.

The emu is an Australian bird that cannot fly, but it can run very fast.

The kookaburra bird's call sounds like a noisy laugh.

Australia is the world's biggest producer of wool.

The native people are called Aborigines, which means "from the beginning."

A didjeridoo is a long, hollow tree branch the Aborigines make into a horn.

Sheepshearers cut the wool off a sheep in one piece.

The Australian greeting is "G'day."

Australians enjoy grilling food on the "barbie," or barbecue.

Aborigines hunted with boomerangs, flat, curved pieces of wood that come back to the thrower.

The kangaroo is a marsupial that hops on strong hind legs, using its long tail for balance.

A young kangaroo is called a joey.

Children in remote areas of the outback listen to school lessons on the radio.

Country	Area sq mi (sq km)	Population	Language	Government	Currency
Australia	2,967,893 (7,686,843)	20,090,437	English	Democracy	Dollar

93

Papua New Guinea

The cities are modern, but in remote villages in Papua New Guinea, homes are made of grass. They have no windows, so mosquitoes are kept out.

A bird of paradise

The bird of paradise is just one of the unusual birds found in Papua New Guinea.

Pidgin is one of about 715 languages spoken in Papua New Guinea. In Pidgin, *pepe* (PEH-pah) means "paper" and *suga* (SOO-gah) is "sugar."

New Guinea is an island split into two countries: Indonesia on the west and Papua New Guinea on the east.

INDONESIA

PAPUA NEW GUINEA

Homes near the water are often built on stilts.

PACIFIC OCEAN

Dugout canoes are used by some for transportation.

PACIFIC OCEAN

Port Moresby ★

A New Guinea tribe once escaped an enemy by hiding in a river. When they came out covered with mud, the enemy thought they were evil spirits and ran away. They are known as Mudmen.

Port Moresby is the capital of Papua New Guinea. It was named after British captain John Moresby in 1873.

Many Papua New Guineans still follow ancient rituals of magic and superstition.

Yams are eaten at almost every meal.

A Singsing is a celebration with feasting and dancing.

Kundu drums are played at ceremonies.

Pigs are an important part of the village life. They are often traded like money and even given names.

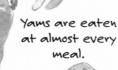

Country	Area sq mi (sq km)	Population	Language	Government	Currency
Papua New Guinea	178,703 (462,841)	5,542,268	Pidgin	Constitutional Monarchy with Parliamentary Democracy	Kina

New Zealand

Rugby is the national sport in New Zealand.

The New Zealand rugby team is called All Blacks.

New Zealand's beautiful countryside is becoming a popular place for making movies.

The Lord of the Rings movies (2001-2003) were filmed in New Zealand.

Maori are the native people of New Zealand. This man wears traditional markings on his face.

New Zealanders often wear a jade stone in a fishhook shape.

Many Maori ceremonies take place where a traditional meeting house sits called a marae.

In New Zealand, there are about 10 sheep for every person.

The tuatara lizard lives in New Zealand. It is a descendant of the dinosaur. It can live up to 77 years.

The kiwi bird is found only in New Zealand. It is so shy, it is seldom seen.

People in New Zealand call themselves Kiwis.

The kiwi bird cannot fly.

Kiwi is also the name of a popular green fruit grown in New Zealand.

Auckland

TASMAN SEA

North Island

Wellington

PACIFIC OCEAN

Christchurch

SOUTHERN ALPS

NEW ZEALAND

Waitaki River

South Island

Dunedin

Country	Area sq mi (sq km)	Population	Language	Government	Currency
New Zealand	104,454 (270,534)	4,035,461	English/Maori	Parliamentary Democracy	Dollar

Antarctica

Weather balloon

Travel in Antarctica is often by snowmobile or dogsled.

At research stations, scientists study weather, fossils, gravity, animal life, and global warming.

A research station

Food and supplies are dropped by plane or helicopter.

All trash must be flown off the continent.

ATLANTIC OCEAN

INDIAN OCEAN

The size of Antarctica is always changing. In the winter, miles of new ice form along the outer rim of the continent. In summer, much of this ice melts away.

Antarctica, the fifth-largest continent, is the coldest, windiest, and driest place on Earth.

The lowest temperatures ever recorded on Earth, -128.6°F (-89.2°C), was on July 21, 1983, at Volstok, the Russian station.

An "icebreaker" is a boat that can charge through the ice. This opens a path for other boats to follow.

WEDDELL SEA

Queen Maud Land

• Ronne Ice Shelf

← N

Vinson Massif 16,066 ft. (4,897 m)

SOUTH POLE ★

Marie Byrd Land

Continent size in summer

• Vostok (Russian research station)

N →

• Magnetic South Pole

• Ross Ice Shelf

Wilkes Land

ROSS SEA

The Antarctic Treaty was signed in 1959. It stated that the continent should only be used for peaceful purposes, including research.

PACIFIC OCEAN

Continent size in winter

N ↓

Antarctic Treaty

Winters in Antarctica are dark and cold. Temperatures almost never rise above 32°F (0°C).

Adélie penguins on parade

A macaroni penguin

Penguins are birds found only in Antarctica. They cannot fly, but they are excellent swimmers.

A king penguin

Chinstrap penguins can be noisy and aggressive.

This is a rockhopper penguin. Rockhoppers have combs like a rooster and red eyes.

Elephant seals have trunks.

Twelve species of whale live in the waters of Antarctica.

This is a baby fur seal. These seals have a visible ear and long flippers. True seals have no outer ear.

This is a blue whale, the largest creature that has ever lived.

Glaciers are enormous ice sheets. They usually move about a foot (0.3048 m) a day.

Often, huge chunks of ice will break off a glacier. These are icebergs, which drift north to warmer seas.

Under all the snow and ice in Antarctica, there is actually land.

An emperor penguin

A Weddell seal

A gentoo penguin and chick

The orca, or killer whale, is ferocious.

Continent	Area sq mi (sq km) summer	Area sq mi (sq km) winter	Population
Antarctica	8,000,000 (20,700,000)	1,000,000 (2,600,000)	Uninhabited

Flags of the World

Afghanistan

Albania

Algeria

Andorra

Angola

Antigua and Barbuda

Argentina

Armenia

Australia

Austria

Azerbaijan

Bahamas

Bahrain

Bangladesh

Barbados

Belarus

Belgium

Belize

Benin

Bhutan

Bolivia

Bosnia-Herzegovina

Botswana

Brazil

Brunei

Bulgaria

Burkina Faso

Burma

Burundi

Cambodia

Cameroon

Canada

Cape Verde

Central African Republic

Chad

Chile

 China

 Colombia

 Comoros

 Congo, Republic of the

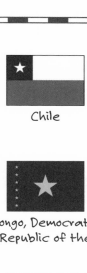 Congo, Democratic Republic of the

 Costa Rica

 Croatia

 Cuba

 Cyprus

 Czech Republic

 Denmark

 Djibouti

 Dominica

 Dominican Republic

 East Timor

 Ecuador

 Egypt

 El Salvador

 Equatorial Guinea

 Eritrea

 Estonia

 Ethiopia

 Fiji

Finland

 France

 Gabon

 Gambia

 Georgia

Germany

 Ghana

 Greece

 Grenada

 Guatemala

Guinea

 Guinea-Bissau

 Guyana

 Haiti

 Honduras

 Hungary

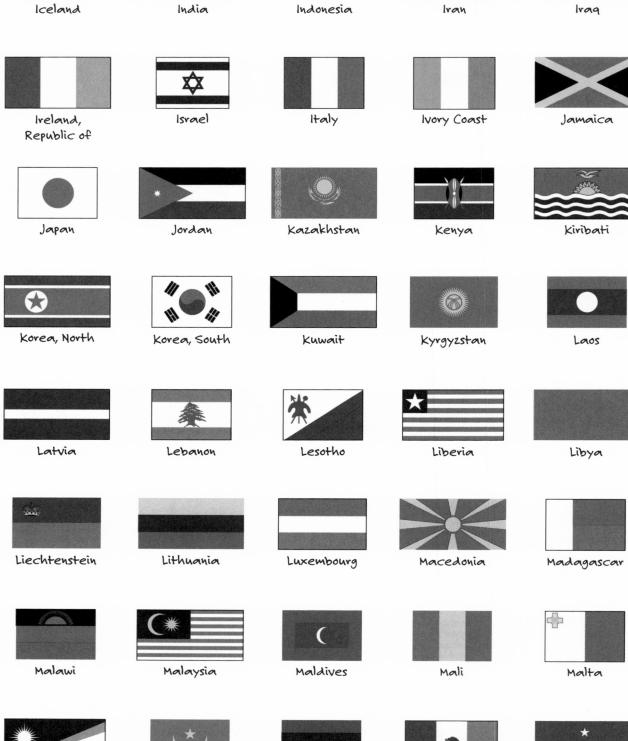

Iceland	India	Indonesia	Iran	Iraq
Ireland, Republic of	Israel	Italy	Ivory Coast	Jamaica
Japan	Jordan	Kazakhstan	Kenya	Kiribati
Korea, North	Korea, South	Kuwait	Kyrgyzstan	Laos
Latvia	Lebanon	Lesotho	Liberia	Libya
Liechtenstein	Lithuania	Luxembourg	Macedonia	Madagascar
Malawi	Malaysia	Maldives	Mali	Malta
Marshall Islands	Mauritania	Mauritius	Mexico	Micronesia

 Moldova

 Monaco

 Mongolia

Morocco

 Mozambique

 Namibia

Nauru

 Nepal

 Netherlands

 New Zealand

 Nicaragua

 Niger

 Nigeria

 Norway

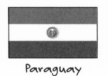 Oman

 Pakistan

 Palau

Panama

 Papua New Guinea

 Paraguay

 Peru

 Philippines

 Poland

 Portugal

 Qatar

 Romania

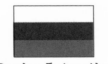 Russian Federation

 Rwanda

 St. Kitts-Nevis

 St. Lucia

 St. Vincent and the Grenadines

 Samoa

 San Marino

 São Tomé and Príncipe

 Saudi Arabia

 Senegal

 Serbia and Montenegro

 Seychelles

 Sierra Leone

 Singapore

 Slovakia

 Slovenia

 Solomon Islands

 Somalia

 South Africa

 Spain

 Sri Lanka

 Sudan

 Suriname

 Swaziland

 Sweden

 Switzerland

 Syria

 Taiwan

 Tajikistan

 Tanzania

 Thailand

 Togo

 Tonga

 Trinidad and Tobago

 Tunisia

 Turkey

 Turkmenistan

 Tuvalu

 Uganda

 Ukraine

 United Arab Emirates

 United Kingdom

 United States of America

 Uruguay

 Uzbekistan

 Vanuatu

 Vatican City

 Venezuela

 Vietnam

 Yemen

 Zambia

Zimbabwe

Index

Index of Continents

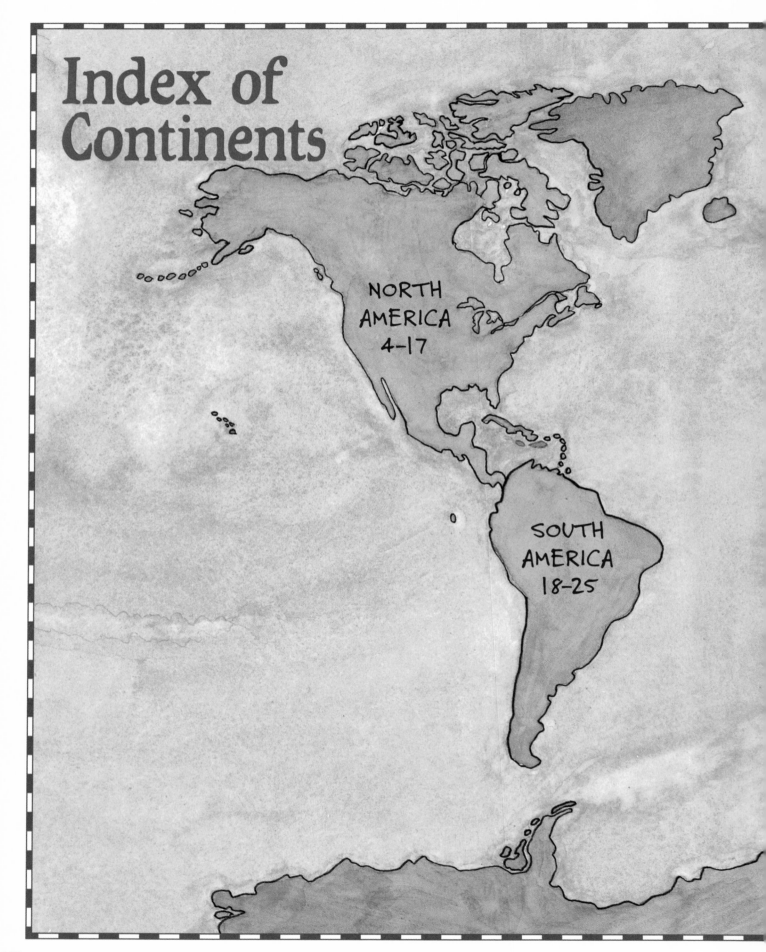

NORTH
AMERICA
4–17

SOUTH
AMERICA
18–25

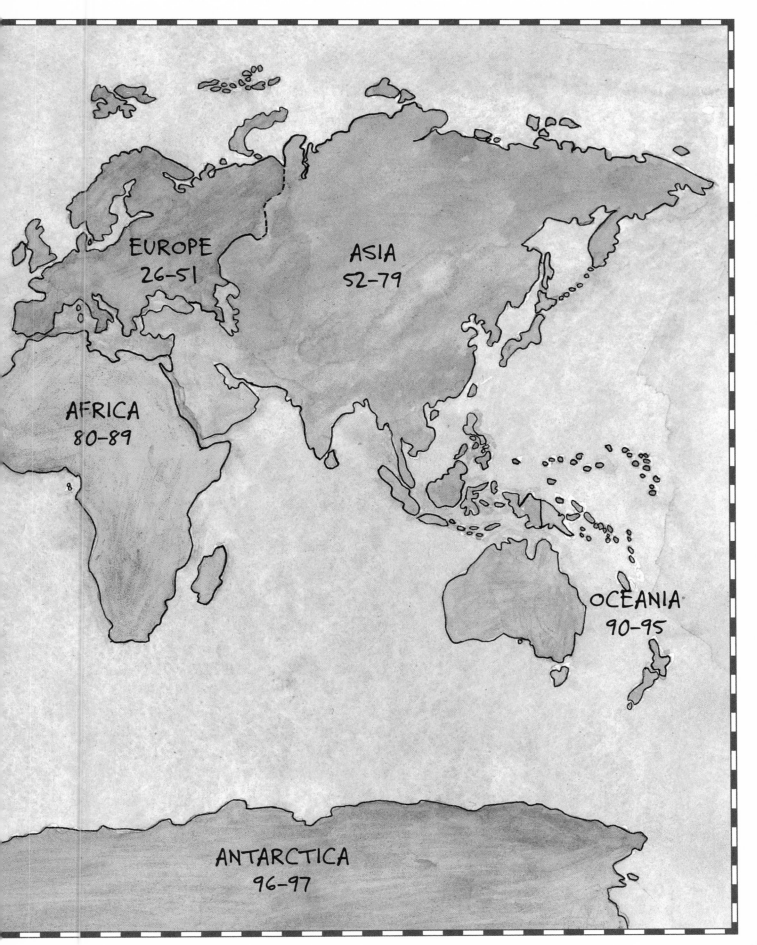

EUROPE
26–51

ASIA
52–79

AFRICA
80–89

OCEANIA
90–95

ANTARCTICA
96–97

Index of Countries